Unidentifie Hyperobject: UFOs, Philosophy, and the End of the World

MW00917513

JAMES D. MADDEN

ONTOCALYPSE PRESS

DEDICATION

For James S. Pappas. My friend who has kept me grounded in the weird for twenty-five years.

CONTENTS

FOREWORD

This book is important—and because it's important, it isn't easy. To put this book in its proper context, I think we need to talk about why both of those things are true. And, somewhat ironically, the reason that it is important, I would argue, is not nearly as important as the reason that it is hard. So let's dispatch with why it's important first.

For a long time now, ufology has been stuck. Once one accepts—or even entertains—the reality of the UFO phenomenon, the very next question that naturally arises is, "Who is inside the UFOs?" Or perhaps, if one is a bit more sophisticated, "What is the nature of the intelligence behind UFOs?" And in the three-quarters of a century that we've had to ask that question, we've come up with a rather limited menu of possibilities, none of which seem to entirely fit the evidence.

In the grand pantheon of things we have considered, they all ultimately break down into a handful of buckets—extraterrestrial, ultraterrestrial, extratempestrial, interdimensional, and for the historically adventurous, a human (or nearly human) breakaway civilization. None are entirely satisfying. All have flaws. And to be frank, very few people seem to be as bothered by this reality as they ought to be.

A popular solution to the lack-of-fit problem that plagues each one of these possible answers to the most basic question that we can ask about UFOs is to say that the phenomenon likely has many causes. Just like in school, when in doubt, most choose to fill in the bubble next to "all of the above." And while that's a viable strategy—and it might even turn out to be correct—we should never confuse the act of hedging our bets with actually knowing the answer. And yet we do, and we do it all the time.

But why do we do that? Why aren't we more curious? It turns out that it isn't a lack of curiosity that is our problem, but an overabundance of it.

In his paper, "The Psychology of Curiosity", George Loewenstein identified four ways of involuntarily inducing curiosity in a human being: (i) the "posing of a question or presentation of a puzzle"; (ii) "exposure to a sequence of events with an anticipated but unknown resolution"; (iii) "the violation of expectations that triggers a search for an explanation"; and (iv) knowledge of "possession of information by someone else." It's hard to think of a phenomenon more perfectly suited to engage our curiosity than that of UFOs (even against our will). And the curiosity that it engenders in us is not idle or passing, but potent and, at times, even distressing.

Curiosity is shaped like a lowercase "n". It's at its weakest when people have no idea about the answer to a question and then again when they are convinced that they do. Curiosity peaks when people think that they might have the answer, but they aren't sure that they do. It's in that tantalizing and

1

maddening zone that the UFO lives, refusing to land.

Journalist Will Storr writes of Loewenstein's research in his book *The Science of Storytelling*:

> "Brain scans reveal that curiosity begins as a little kick in the brain's reward system: we crave to know the answer, or what happens next in the story, in the way we might crave drugs or sex or chocolate. This pleasantly unpleasant state, that causes us to squirm with tantalised discomfort at the delicious promise of an answer, is undeniably powerful. During one experiment, psychologists noted archly that their participants' 'compulsion to know the answer was so great that they were willing to pay for the information, even though curiosity could have been sated for free after the session.'"

Our desire to know the answer causes us to imagine that we have answers where there are none, just to take the edge off. As James Madden himself would be quick to point out, this tendency is part of what it means to be cave-dwellers in the Platonic sense. And because the curiosity inflicted upon us by the irresolvability of the paradoxes surrounding the UFO phenomenon is so great, those who are engaged in its study ought to be more aware of this pitfall. If ever we catch ourselves feeling too comfortable, it should be a sign to us that we have stopped thinking.

What Madden offers us with this book is a new way forward. We've been in need of new ideas—and not just another not-quite-right category to line up on the shelf alongside the others, but ideas that have the ability to collapse the existing categories and resolve them into a more holistic and coherent model. The UFO as a (potentially hybrid) hyperobject does exactly that. It doesn't give us any definitive answers, but it gives us a way to think about UFOs that doesn't force us to overcommit to premises we can't defend or reduce its more confounding aspects to fit the contours of our well-worn tropes. It's progress, the likes of which we haven't seen for decades.

But this book isn't just about *what* we should think about the UFO phenomenon, but *how* we should think about it—or about anything, really. Like any great teacher, Madden's aim here is not to give us a fish, but to teach us to fish. By showing how he arrived at his novel and ingenious Uber-Umwelt Terrestrial Hypothesis (UUTH), he demonstrates how one can think their way into the very heart of this problem—and back out again into a new world. And in exposing our epistemic vulnerabilities, he makes clear the level of intellectual discipline, rigor, and humility that it takes to do so, which is anything but easy.

This book is a challenge to the UFO community, and in some ways, even an indictment of it. And if that makes us uncomfortable, I'd suggest that it's because he has a point. Most of the discourse in the UFO community centers around disclosure, transparency, government cover-ups, and whistleblower revelations. We rail against gatekeepers. We demand answers. But in the tradition of great ufological thinkers—like Vallée, Keel, and Pasulka—whose message is too-often lost on the very community that most needs to hear it, what Madden is showing us with this book is that we are our own gatekeepers. We are the thing that keeps us from getting at the truth, and we're better at it than any shadowy government entity ever could be.

The reality of the UFO takes a wrecking ball to our consensus reality. It breaks all of our models. It smashes all of our paradigms. It's the harbinger of an ontological apocalypse that calls everything into question. Which is why, in many ways, to demand that someone give us the answers about UFOs is to miss the point entirely. There is nothing that the President could say from a podium that will be sufficient to piece the world back together again. Any answer that would actually make sense to us in our current state could only ever be a lie. The revolution will not be televised, because it can't be. There is no passive way to receive this information. You can't be told—*but you can know*.

Plato's allegory of the Cave is both about how this kind of education can occur, and a means for starting the process. It's both the map and the shovel for digging your way out. It is because of the Cave that I met two of my greatest teachers, James Madden and Diana Pasulka, and I'm so grateful for the role that they have played in helping me to understand it. It took time, and it wasn't easy. I read *Republic*, in which the allegory of the Cave appears, and then I read it again. I read Heidegger and Nietzsche and Debord. I read Vallée and Keel and Kripal and Pasulka. I read Hoffman and Morton. I spent hours sitting by the lake near my home, staring out at the water. And after a year and a half of reading, thinking, and writing about the Cave, and having literally hundreds of conversations about it with people around the world—and with Jim, in particular—I'm finally satisfied that I know what it means.

In preparing to write this foreword, I went back and found the very first email that I sent to Diana with my questions about the Cave. She graciously replied to me, but, to be honest, at the time I didn't really understand her answer. It felt like a riddle that I needed to solve. I was grateful for the help and the direction, but I also just sort of wished she'd come out with it already. Finding that email again, I laughed until I had tears running down my face because she did tell me what the Cave was in that email. In one sentence, as clear as day, she wrote: "It is a mystical transmission that is cultivated through extreme critical thought, and engaged in with others."

That is the answer, but at the time I didn't have "ears to hear" or "eyes to see." I had no way of knowing back then how that simple answer could be infinitely unfolded like a hyperdimensional Swiss army knife—how it could be used as a tool that can help you find the answer to any question worth asking if you're willing to engage in the work of becoming a thing that can know it.

I will warn you that this work is not for the faint of heart. The process of coming to see the Cave is traumatic, the light outside the Cave is obliterating, and upon returning to the Cave below, the prisoner finds that all their past concerns are now meaningless, and that they have become unintelligible to everyone still inside. The self-annihilation and alienation inherent in that process can only be undertaken by those who are made of tougher stuff.

It's exactly that kind of education that Madden offers us with *Unidentified Flying Hyperobject*. This book isn't a long one. You could read it in one sitting. And yet, unless you're already a trained philosopher, one read-through likely won't be enough for you to apprehend its meaning—because, to be clear, these are the kinds of thoughts that one apprehends as opposed to comprehends. Ideas like these can't be absorbed passively like the proverbial mustard seed falling onto freshly plowed ground. Even the most well-prepared mind is going to have to chase them down.

If there is anything that I have learned from Jim's example, it's that the life of a philosopher is not a peaceful one of planting and cultivation. To be a philosopher is to be a warrior—a hunter. To feed your mind requires that you only eat what you kill. If you're doing it right, there will be blood.

Kelly Chase
November 2023

The sense of the world must lie outside the world. In the world everything is as it is and everything happens as it does happen. In it there is no value—and if there were, it would be of no value.

—Ludwig Wittgenstein, *Tractatus Logico-Philosophicus*[1]

There is a natural tendency to concentrate on only those facets which seem most interesting, or which provide the best evidence. The phenomenon of unidentified flying objects is a gigantic iceberg, and the truly important aspects are hidden far beneath the surface.

—John Keel, *Operation Trojan Horse*[2]

---

[1] Ludwig Wittgenstein, *Tratatus Logicus-Philosophicus*, trans. C.K. Ogden, In *Major Works: Selected Philosophical Writings* (New York: Harper, 2009), §6.41.
[2] John Keel, *Operation Trojan Horse: The Classic Breakthrough Study of UFOs* (San Antonio, TX: Anomalist Press, 1970/2013), p. 1.

INTRODUCTION:
Taking All The Pieces Seriously

"The aim of philosophy, abstractly formulated, is to understand how things in the broadest possible sense of the term hang together in the broadest possible sense of the term. Under 'things in the broadest possible sense' I include such radically different items as not only 'cabbages and kings', but numbers and duties, possibilities and finger snaps, aesthetic experience and death. To achieve success in philosophy would be, to use a contemporary turn of phrase, to 'know one's way around' with respect to all these things, not in that unreflective way in which the centipede of the story knew its way around before it faced the question, 'How do I walk?', but in that reflective way which means that no intellectual holds are barred."

—Wilfrid Sellars, "Philosophy and the Scientific Image of Man"[3]

This book is mostly a cautionary tale aimed, in particular, at counseling humility. The UFO stretches us to—and maybe even beyond—the limits of what humans can understand. Thus, as we approach the Phenomenon, we should mistrust ourselves simultaneously as we try to make sense of it.

The UFO takes us into territory that our minds probably have not been designed to map, so any conclusion we come to has to be handled with suspicion. As always, restraint is needed when it comes to the characteristic human presumption to assume we have things pretty much figured. Understanding the UFO is no place to jump to hasty conclusions.

That is correct, but the worry goes deeper. The UFO doesn't only challenge our patience for resisting easy answers, but the very categories fundamental to human thinking and understanding. The UFO reveals just how little it seems we are fit to understand about the world, and it should therefore occasion us to reflect on the consequences of our finitude. Understanding something that seems to indicate our very grounds for understanding are insufficient for building a comprehensive perspective is a deep irony to fall into—but here we are confronting just such a phenomenon. By putting the UFO into question, we put ourselves, as thinkers and knowers, into question. In the following pages, I will attempt to hone some explanatory tools for understanding that are sensitive to the fact that the UFO cannot help but to shake our confidence in our ability to understand.

---

[3] Willfred Sellars, "Philosophy and the Scientific Image of Man," in *Science, Perception, and Reality* (Atascadero, CA: Ridgeview Publishing, 1991), 1.

Before beginning that task, I need to follow my own counsel of humility with respect to the ufological community. I am a post-2017 UFO freak. Before that, I was just another college professor, teaching classic authors and writing about standard academic issues in the philosophy of mind and the philosophy of religion.

As an almost cliché Gen-Xer, I spent a lot of time in college watching the *X-Files*. Though I always found it believable that somebody like the Smoking Man killed JFK (my dad came back from Vietnam with enough stories to give me a healthy mistrust, and Oliver Stone certainly helped me along too), I could never quite go with Fox Mulder when it came to the alien conspiracy. Later, I was intrigued by the bombshell tidings in the *The New York Times* and other things about the UFO I heard on the *Joe Rogan Experience*, but nothing really moved the needle.

That all changed when I was working through the *X-Files* with my kids (I've seen to it that they have been exposed to the finer things) as the infamous Pentagon briefing happened in June of 2021. It looked to me as though the official line had just done a 180-degree turn. Whereas for the last seventy-five years we had been told "There's nothing to see here," now they are saying "Well, maybe there is something . . . ." Was Mulder right?

On top of that, this change in acceptable discourse about the UFO transpired in the middle of some of the strangest years in recent history. That started me down the proverbial rabbit hole, and as a dispositional "book guy" I began to read everything I could get my hands on. I'm sure most of you reading this have traveled that same pathway, so I won't go through that material in detail—and those of you new to the UFO issue will find plenty of references in the coming pages.

I was deeply moved first by how good the evidence really is for the UFO phenomenon. As someone trained in the philosophy of religion, I was struck, in particular, by the fact that the evidence for the reality of the UFO (whatever it is) is *at least* as good as the evidence supporting the founding miracles of the major religious traditions. Whatever you think about those particular claims, I don't believe they completely lack evidential support, i.e., the traditional miracle claims have enough going for themselves evidentially that they cannot be ruled out.[4] If that is the case, then it seems like we can't

---

[4] My view is that the evidence for the traditional miracle claims is enough that they cannot be ruled out, but not strong enough to justify "betting your life on it." Thus, there is some sort of act of faith on the part of believers in these miracles. For what I take to be the best account of evidential concerns in philosophy of religion, see Thomas Sullivan and Sandra Menssen, *The Agnostic Inquirer: Revelation from a Philosophical Standpoint* (Grand Rapids, MI: Eerdmans, 2007).

rule out UFOs either—and given the continued frequency and quality of UFO reports, there are very good grounds to rule them in.

Even if you think the case for religious miracles is utterly without support, the fact that so many people, who are otherwise very rational, believe in these events is itself a significant datum that requires an account in our general understanding of things. This is also the case for the UFO: even if you doubt the evidential credentials supporting the belief, the fact that it is so widely held begs for some sort of explanation in terms of the structure of the human psyche.[5]

There are many things that masses of people believe that have evidential parity with the reports of UFOs. For example, the evidence for the assassination of Bin Laden and the Tic Tac UFO from the *Nimitz* incident are at least equally as strong. In both cases we just have the testimony of certain experts and purported witnesses.

Moreover, given the on-going nature of reported UFO appearances, in many cases the UFO claims have even more support than some common, uncontroversial beliefs. The reason the latter are typically taken as within the bounds of reason and the former beyond the fringe, is a dispositional belief conservatism—when in doubt, don't revise the basics!—we all have that biases us against claims that don't fit our going-consensus picture of reality. At some point, however, the evidence can accumulate to the point that the "anomalous" has to be given a place in the "ordinary." I became convinced that the UFO has achieved that status.

I also found that the further I got into the UFO question, the more other, more familiar questions about the nature and limitations of the human mind kept cropping up. The problem of the UFO has a great deal of resonance with the philosophical problems I have spent my professional life (and personal life, too) pondering for the last thirty years.

In short, a theory of the UFO is going to have significant consequences for your theory of everything. Taking the phenomenon seriously will change how you think of a lot of other things—maybe everything. I found that accommodating the UFO both shed light on and darkened the deepest questions about the mind and metaphysics that have always fascinated me.

When I happened upon Diana Pasulka's pioneering book, *American Cosmic: UFOs, Religion, Technology*, I had in my hands an example of philosophically sophisticated academic work on the UFO that covered much the same territory as my own thinking. With Pasulka as an example, I set to work on the UFO as an object of formal philosophical inquiry, dedicating a

---

[5] This is one of many invaluable points that Jung makes in his classic, *Flying Saucers: A Modern Myth of Things Seen in the Skies*, trans. R.F.C. Hull (Princeton, N.J.: Princeton University Press, 1978).

lot of my research efforts to this issue. I even raised a few eyebrows at my religiously conservative day job when I taught a course on the UFO and the epistemology of religious myth. The results of that research and teaching, for what they are worth, are what I have to show you in this book.

I am a *Johnny-come-lately* to the ufology scene. I only got involved once it became "OK" in the mainstream (or at least less stigmatized) to take up this topic. There were many very bright, very dedicated people working on this issue for dozens of years. A lot of these researchers did admirably disciplined scholarship, and the work cost them much in terms of mainstream prestige (and without all the benefits of an academic position—time and tenure). Until very recently I, too, was dismissive of what they were up to. For that I am now sorry. I am, at best, only a member of the second wave of academics working in the humanities and social sciences who have jumped into this arena. The mantle of the *avant garde* for academic ufology in the humanities and social sciences goes to Diana Pasulka, Jeffrey Kripal, and their associates and students.

Again, I am in the debt of these trailblazers. These facts need to be emphasized at the outset, because I will have some sharp things to say about ufology as it currently stands. But please note that these critical claims come from an overall stance of gratitude for keeping this issue, and its associated literature, alive through the dark ages of stigmatization while articulating irreplaceable insights into the phenomenon. Scholarship always involves the odd circumstance of standing on other people's shoulders even as you criticize them for the way they are supporting you.

I should also make clear upfront that I have no direct insight into the UFO phenomenon. I am not a spy in from the cold or military veteran with secrets to tell, nor am I an experiencer. I have no intelligence connections, and I have never encountered a UFO (to my recollection). I also have not spent time, beyond reading the standard ufological literature, surveying or interviewing people who have those sorts of experiences or access to such information. I have no scoop on the latest behind-the-scenes machinations or bizarre encounters. You will not find any predictions in these pages regarding when or how disclosure will happen. I am neither a physicist nor an engineer, so don't think I am going to give you some insights into how alien technology might actually work or whether a warp drive is a physical possibility.

All of that is important, but as a philosopher none of it is in my purview—however much I, too, find those topics to be fascinating. The enquiry you are about to begin is *philosophical*, not *historical, political, journalistic*, or *scientific*. As a philosophical exercise, this inquiry is not going to uncover some previously unknown fact. Philosophers are not the ones who will find out what really happened at Roswell or discover how anti-gravity propulsion works. There is a sense in which philosophers (when we behave ourselves and stay in our disciplinary lane) don't ever discover anything new at all. That's the work of scientists, historians, and other types of scholars.

Since a philosophical inquiry (in the narrow, professional, academic sense) is off the beaten path of ufology and comes at some expense (our discussion of Plato, Aristotle, Heidegger, and other philosophical luminaries will require effort on your part), it is fair to wonder what is to be gained by the trouble. What does a philosopher suppose he can contribute to ufology, if he admits that his work will not uncover anything new?

Return to how Wilfrid Sellars defines "the aim of philosophy" in the quotation I offer above: "to understand how things in the broadest possible sense of the term hang together in the broadest possible sense of the term." Here, too, we see that philosophy adds no new *things*, but understands how things *hang together*. The philosopher attempts to gain, as Sellars puts it elsewhere in the same essay, a "synoptic view of the whole."

We have various disciplines,—e.g., chemistry, religious studies, history, etc.—each of which makes discoveries within certain recesses of the world. Notice, however, the more the chemist, the religious scholar, and the historian start to ask what chemistry, religion, and history have to do with each other, the less they are thinking specifically as chemists, religious scholars, or historians. In fact, to the degree they are able to make sense of their specialized sciences in light of each other, they are beginning to think in very much the same way.

The idealized version of this thinking of all the disciplines together is philosophy. That is, the philosopher attempts to put all the pieces of our various modes of understanding into a coherent picture of the world. What is the world like such that chemistry, religion, and history all have something to say about it? The philosopher doesn't add puzzle pieces but tries to piece together what is already provided by the specialists.

To put it with a bit of grandiosity, the philosopher answers the proverbial question "What does it all mean?" in the sense of speculating what the meaningful whole composed by all the parts of our knowledge might be. Even if there is no such meaningful whole, that is an answer to the question, and one a philosopher should entertain. Maybe things don't hang together very well or at least how they hang together is not within the human grasp!

Once again, as Sellars rightly claimed, philosophical sense-making is "no holds barred," so we can't presume a happy ending to our inquiry from the beginning. That might even mean that a philosopher could come to the conclusion that philosophy is not really a possibility—there isn't a synoptic view for the philosopher to articulate. As you will see in the following pages, such an irony about philosophy and the human condition is one of the suggestions of the UFO phenomenon.

Philosophy is also "no holds barred" in the sense that it doesn't ignore any of the available puzzle pieces in attempting to construct the synoptic view. As Sellars puts it, "not only 'cabbages and kings', but numbers and duties, possibilities and finger snaps, aesthetic experience and death" however difficult they might be to fit into the picture currently in vogue.

I believe the time has come that academic philosophy cannot ignore that the UFO is a significant piece to the puzzle, and we will fail in our role as the synthesizer of the disciplines as long as we continue to set it aside. In any event, I hope your efforts in following this inquiry produce something closer to that synoptic vision, however far we finally fall short of the true view of the whole (and we always do fall short).

Another function of philosophy, and one that might be more interesting to specialists working on the nitty-gritty of the UFO question, is to propose models based on the synoptic view. Philosophy does not verify hypotheses. We don't make new discoveries in that sense. We can, however, propose models incorporating specific phenomena into a much broader context that the relevant specialists may put to the test.

Philosophers are removed from actual empirical verification of our claims. We are more apt to think about what is possible rather than what is actual, i.e., *what could be the case* as opposed to *what really is the case*. The downside of that untethering from the actual is that philosophers, quite famously, have proposed some wildly speculative things. For example, I wrote my dissertation on G.W. Leibniz, a seventeenth century philosopher and mathematician (he co-discovered calculus with Newton) who argues that all of reality can be reduced to thoughts in an infinity of self-contained souls!

Yes, that is *prima facie* crazy, but Leibniz's reasons are not as easily dismissed as you might like, and what he claims is possible in the broadest sense of logical possibility (as opposed to physical possibility). He also proposed his idealist-atomism (what he called his monadology) as a way of making sense of both modern physics and consciousness in a single synoptic picture of reality.

As the history of science and consciousness studies have progressed, these kinds of idealist views have started to take on the air of promising hypotheses for those particular sciences.[6] I'm not coming out for Leibniz here (though I'm not sure he's wrong either), but the point is that today's wild philosophical speculation, when done with logical rigor and informed by the best available insights from across the disciplines, can become tomorrow's serious scientific hypothesis.

In the following pages, I am going to do a bit of wild philosophical speculation regarding the UFO, with the hopes that these proposals might

---

[6] You can find good examples along these lines in Philip Goff, *Galileo's Error: Foundations for a New Science of Consciousness* (New York: Vintage, 2009) and Bernardo Kastrup, *The Idea of the World: A Multi-Disciplinary Argument for the Mental Nature of Reality* (New York: IFF Books, 2019).

give the relevant specialists some ideas of where to go looking for discoveries. But those actual discoveries are not something I can produce from the comfort of the philosopher's armchair. Intellectual progress is a team sport.

So here is the plan for what follows. In the first part of the book, *Plato, Aristotle, and Our Contact with the World Beyond* I put some insights of classical philosophy into a conversation with recent work in cognitive science, the humanities, and ufology. Chapter 1, *Cave Dwelling, Memory, and the UFO* begins with an account of the structures of cognition that both enable and limit human understanding, i.e., relevance sorting, social conformity, and technological extension. I couple these notions with insights drawn from Plato's *Republic* to make the case that necessary conditions of understanding entail that there is much of which we are irredeemably ignorant outside of our cognitive cave. We then turn to Whitley Strieber's most recent work for concrete examples of "trans-cave" experiences, with particular emphasis on the role both he and Plato put on *memory* as our access to the world beyond. The discussion will introduce principles of cognitive limitation and humility that will be integral to all of our subsequent discussions.

Chapter 2, *Aristotle, Myth, and Extraterrestrial Intelligences: An Ancient 'Super Natural' Philosophy of Religion*, introduces Aristotle's natural theology. On this view, nature is an interlocking hierarchy of "intelligibilities" (deities) governed by ascending relations of admiration, terminating at the highest level in *the god*, Aristotle's fabled "unmoved mover." The point of this chapter is not to defend Aristotle's natural theology, but to see how he thinks without our modern distinction between *natural* and *supernatural*, for Aristotle, *nature is super*—its runs on divinity suffused throughout its various cosmological layers.

I see here an ancient anticipation of Kripal's notion of "Super Nature", which is a very useful concept for us to have in mind as we go forward. Moreover, Aristotle's natural theology will play an important role in understanding my development of Vallée's "Control Hypothesis" in a later chapter. Aristotle is also sensitive to how religious myth can be both a vehicle for insight into Super Nature and a means of manipulation and confusion. That Janus-faced character of religious myth will also be important for our subsequent discussions, especially when we confront Pasulka's work in the final part of the book.

Part 2, *Super Nature and Ontology Beyond the Cave: The Metaphysics of the UFO* is where I attempt a speculative and synoptic account of the phenomenon. I begin in chapter 3, *UFO Realism and the Uber-Umwelt: A Model for a Revised Ultraterrestrial Hypothesis* by first pointing to a probability shortcoming standard extraterrestrial and ultraterrestrial models suffer—and here I mostly draw on Jacques Vallée's work. I then introduce a concept taken from phenomenology and cognitive science, the *Umwelt*. This notion, which fits well with the Platonic and Aristotelian ideas I develop in Part 1, is built around the highly selective nature of our perceptual and cognitive apparatus, such that we build an "environment" for ourselves (*Umwelt*) by leaving a far more complicated and richer world "out there" in the *Uber-Umwelt*, beyond our ken. We then consider that the UFO, along with a lot of other "spooky" stuff, might not be alien creatures or a breakaway civilization, but "nearby" beings that exist just outside our conveniently constructed *Umwelt*. When we run into such things, they are uncanny and don't make sense.

In chapter 4, *Unidentified Flying Hyperobject: Thinking Beyond the Goldilocks Ontology*, I develop this hypothesis by drawing on Graham Harman's object oriented ontology and Timothy Morton's related development of the notion of a hyperobject. The point of this chapter is to challenge the reader to think outside the cave a bit—what I call our "Goldilocks Ontology."

The proposal here is that the UFO is not the many, disparate things that barely show up in our *Umwelt*, but one gigantic thing, a hyperobject, existing on a scale and complexity that defies our understanding in the *Uber-Umwelt*. As we will see, this proposal, however wildly speculative, helps make sense of the apparent fact that our activities since 1945 have somehow catalyzed the phenomenon, while suggesting that we have much to learn about ourselves as we examine it. I will also suggest that the idea of the UFO as a hyperobject gives us reason to question the dichotomy between the artificial and the natural, just as we have grounds to collapse the opposition between natural and the supernatural.

I use chapter 5, *Magonia as Hyperobject: The Organic Control Hypothesis and the Re-Enchantment of the World*, to synthesize my speculations with what I take to be the most plausible ontological model for the UFO extant in current ufology, Vallée's "Control Hypothesis." I argue that we should understand Vallée's notion of a system of control as something like a hyperobject, though I make the case that we should understand it on an analogy with an organism, which I think is implicit in Vallée's original theory. The fact that this control system, according to Vallée, operates by manipulating us cognitively (through mythology/de-mythology) invokes Aristotle's natural theology, or so I will argue in this chapter.

The work of Diana Pasulka takes centerstage in Part 3, *The UFO and the End of the World: Thinking After American Cosmic*. Here I am particularly keen to draw out the Nietzschean and Heideggerian themes in her contribution to ufology. Chapter 6, *The UFO, Religion, and Our Epistemic Vulnerability: Diana Pasulka's Unheard Message for Ufology*, may be the most controversial moment in this book. My main argument here is that mainstream ufology has fundamentally misunderstood the central message about ufology that Pasulka is offering. Namely, she makes a very strong case that ufology is a sort of religion, and like any religion it is subject to destabilizing Nietzschean critiques. Moreover, this potential Nietzschean debunking is all the more threatening today, given the power of digital media to displace our relationship to reality. That is a key lesson from *American Cosmic* for ufology, and religion in general, and I try to make it explicit in this chapter.

Finally, in chapter 7, *Apocalyptic Philosophizing: Jacques Vallée as the Oppenheimer of the Digital Age*, I turn to Pasulka's sparse but philosophically pregnant appeals to Heidegger in *American Cosmic*. She begins and ends her book by invoking Heidegger, and in doing so she identifies Vallée as a sort of personification of a key moment in his thought. I draw out these claims by offering an extended interpretation of Heidegger's *Question Concerning Technology*, emphasizing how it can help us find the place the UFO plays in the synoptic vision of the whole, though Heidegger sees the broad picture as fraught with danger.

Along the way, I make the case that Oppenheimer is a personification of Heidegger's thought for the Atomic Age, and that will allow us to understand how Vallée is such for the digital age. Both scientists are thinking of our greatest danger and our greatest hope as constitutive of a self-imposed apocalypse. In Vallée's case, through his work with the UFO mystery, the possibility of something speaking to us through this grave threat is near to hand. For me, this is one of the primary fascinations evoked by the UFO, and thus the work of understanding Heidegger in application to the phenomenon is essential.

Part 1:
Plato, Aristotle, and Our Contact with the World Beyond

1 Cave Dwelling, Memory, and the UFO

"The subject has to be seen as having a 'life' in all the rich senses of this word—as formed by its individual history, as a living bodily subject of experience, and as belonging to an intersubjective 'life-world.'"

—Evan Thompson, *Mind in Life*[7]

"Our experience is the same: living in a certain hollow of the earth, we believe that we lived upon its surface; the air we call the heavens, as if the stars made their way through it; this too is the same: because in our weakness and slowness we are not able to make our way to the upper limit of the air; if anyone got to this upper limit, if anyone came to it or reached it on wings and his head rose above it, then just as fish on rising from the sea see things in our region, he would see things there and, if his nature could endure to contemplate them, he would know that there is the true heaven, the true light and the true earth, for the earth here, these stones and the whole region, are spoiled and eaten away, just as things in the sea are by salt water."

—Plato, *Phaedo*[8]

"I think that it was a critically important insight. Rather than say, 'This woman

---

[7] Evan Thompson, *Mind in Life: Biology, Phenomenology, and the Sciences of Mind* (Cambridge, MA: Harvard University Press, 2007), 30.

[8] Plato, *Phaedo*, translated by G.M.A. Grube, in *Plato: Complete Works* (Indianapolis, IN: Hackett Publishing, 1987), 94.

remembered being abducted by aliens,' we are better off asking. 'Why did this woman end up with this memory, and what does it mean about human experience?'"

Whitley Strieber, *Them.*[9]

We will get to the UFO eventually, but I need to beg your patience first. As I mentioned in the preface to this book, I want to slow us down. We need to *think* about the UFO anew, from the ground up. The UFO phenomenon is always confusing, often unprecedented (at least with respect to "common sense"), and, at times, utterly destabilizing. It forces us to think our way out to the very limits of our cognitive powers. Indeed, when we are dealing with the UFO, we are often required to speculate in ways that may in fact take us beyond the edges of what can be made sense of by human beings, and drawing out the consequences of that fact will be part of the central concern of this book.

Since the UFO demands that we think out beyond the pale of our usual sense-making procedures, it lends itself to more than the usual risks of misinterpretation and even outright distortion that come along with any of our experiences and subsequent attempts at understanding. Thus, when I talk about rethinking the UFO "from the ground up," my primary concern is not to make a fresh assessment of the available empirical evidence. As we discussed earlier, that's not a philosopher's job, and we philosophers only get ourselves into trouble when we meddle in such affairs. I will happily leave those worries to the scientists and historians.

Rather, our task here is to *rethink how we think about the* UFO. If the UFO takes us to our very cognitive limits (or maybe, paradoxically, beyond our limits), then our understanding of the UFO needs to begin with some grasp of the cognitive box that frames all our thinking. In other words, I want to rethink the UFO in light of what we know about the limitations of human thinking. That can help us better understand, at least, what we don't know about the UFO, or maybe even *can't* know about the UFO.

Moreover, reflecting on the UFO in this way, i.e., beginning with an articulation of the limitations of human thinking, will at least occasion our reflection about our human situation. That is, even if our attempts to understand the UFO end in an obscure opacity, they may nevertheless lead to a greater transparency with respect to ourselves by forcing us to face the limitations of our human lot. Indeed, as we will see throughout the following discussion, my view is that the primary benefit of reflecting on the UFO phenomenon is to disabuse us of much of our humanistic pretensions. By contemplating the UFO, we might become better acquainted with ourselves, at

---

[9] Whitely Streiber, *Them.* (San Antonio, TX: Walker and Collier, 2023)

least in coming to terms with what we can't know.

There are a lot of aspects of human cognition to be taken into account, but I will focus on three primary structures of human experience and sense-making that both enable and limit our thinking (really, they enable our thinking by limiting our thinking) in ways that, as we shall see, are salient with respect to how we approach the UFO. These three limits of thinking are: (a) *relevance sorting*, (b) *social conformity*, and (c) *techno-cognitive extension*. I will begin with relevance sorting.

Consider even the most mundane conversation you might have with a casual acquaintance. In such a situation, how many true statements could you make? In the room you are meeting there might be tables, chairs, smart phones, welding tools, plants, and other human beings. There are most definitely microscopic organisms (germs!) and invisible gasses (hopefully enough oxygen, and not too much carbon-dioxide), along with all sorts of whirring and buzzing (birds chirping outside, a ventilation fan making just barely audible sounds). Maybe there are mice or other critters living in the walls. According to our going scientific theories, there are also vast multitudes of subatomic particles whirling around the space we identify as the room, which are in various levels of organization. Moreover, we might even recognize (and I will make a case for as much in a later chapter) that there are also much "bigger" things like the Institutional Review Board, the Internal Revenue Service, the economy, and the environment that are present in the room, at least through their effects.

Suppose I've gone to the room to meet with a colleague to discuss our plans for a joint business venture. In such a situation, it is certainly *true* that "There are germs on the surface of the desk," "There is happily ample enough oxygen in the room," and "The particles composing my chair are bonded into a lattice structure," but making any of those utterances would likely earn me a quizzical look from my friend. In fact, she would likely point out to me that I have *stopped making sense*! Moreover, if I persist in this way, she might further conclude, with good reason, that I had begun to lose my grip on reality.

The point is not that my utterances are false, as if I were to declare myself to be made out of glass, but that I had lost my ability to understand what is *relevant*. In doubting my sanity, my friend would not be doubting that there are germs on the desk, there is ample oxygen in the room, or the lattice structure of the particles composing my chair. No, she would worry that I have lost my grip on things because I had lost my ability *to sort the things according to what is relevant or irrelevant according to the task at hand*.

That is, our grasp on reality is not merely constituted by our ability to make true statements, but to make true statements that are relevant to some conversational situation. The point is that our cognition always involves an implicit simplification. In order for us to say (or think) something cognitively significant, we must first be able to leave out what is irrelevant to our situation. Our thinking is always a way of carving something out from a much more complex (or even chaotic) whole. As Hubert Dreyfus puts it, "most of what we experience must remain in the background so that something can be perceived in the foreground."[10]

Notice that Dreyfus's point is a general insight into all human thought and cognizable experience, i.e., it only occurs in the context of a prior sorting for relevance. Furthermore, relevance is determined by our ordinary tasks and priorities (the fact that we have come together to discuss a business venture or to celebrate our anniversary), but also by what is generally relevant to our cultural and biological histories:

> It has to do with the way man is at home in his world, has it comfortably wrapped around him, so to speak. Human beings are somehow already situated in such a way that what they need in order to cope with things is distributed around them where they need it . . . This system of relations which makes it possible to discover objects when they are needed is our home or our world. The Human world . . is prestructured in terms of human purposes and concerns in such a way that what counts as an object or is significant about an object is a function of, or embodies, that concern.[11]

In other words, human cognition (and cognizable experience) only occurs in a "world" of pre-given meanings, pragmatic projects, and prior biological-evolutionary conditioning.

Moreover, our emotional state and history makes a difference, too, e.g., I am attuned to all sorts of things during my walk home on a dark night that I would have missed, if I were not so fearful. We need an emotional context to bring certain things into the foreground for us. All of this is to say that we must, as many phenomenological philosophers have put it, have a "world" that is already there *for us* as a precondition for any sensible experience (and subsequent cognition).[12]

---

[10] Hubert Dreyfus, *What Computers Still Can't Do: A Critique of Artificial Reason* (Cambridge, MA: MIT Press, 1982), p. 240.

[11] Ibid., pp. 260-261.

[12] Much of this discussion is following insights that were first developed in the phenomenological philosophy of Martin Heidegger (see *Being and Time*, trans John Macquarrie and Edward Robinson (New York: Harper Collins, 1962)) and Maurice Merleau-Ponty (see *The Phenomenology of Perception*, trans Donald A. Landes (New York, Routledge, 2012)), which were later put to work in cognitive science. See also Andy Clark, *Being There: Putting Brain, Body, and World Together* (Cambridge, MA: Bradford Books, 1997); John Haugland, *Dasein*

That is, we have to have prior projects, commitments, emotional attachments, cultural framings, and biological grounding before we can have a coherent experience. All of these factors narrow down the myriad of possibilities for thought and experience into a package that we can work with. We don't start just simply open to whatever is out there, but with a set of dispositions that prioritize certain elements in our immediate environment over others based on what we are trying to deal with.

This world that frames our experiences and subsequent cognitions, our *Lebenswelt* or "lifeworld" as it is often called in the philosophical literature, is ultimately a simplification that leaves behind much that is not *relevant to us*. In a sense then, what we experience bears our own image, since it has been selected for its relevance to *our concerns and dispositions*. Our world is real, but it is a real world that has been selected for the sake of our convenience relative to our projects. *Relevance* is always *relevance to us*, so it is difficult for us to make any sense of what might be "out there" beyond our "world" that is not relevant to us, though no less real in its own right.

We turn now to *social conformity*. We tend to think of humanity as cognitively significant primarily because of our ability to "think for ourselves,"—to be innovative and independent in our thinking. Though independence of thought does have much to do with our distinctively human standing, the fact of the matter is that human cognition has as much to do with conformity and trust for authority as it does with our ability to go our own way.

Return for a moment to our notion of relevance sorting as a precondition for human cognition. The "world" for which we need to limit the options for experience and cognition is necessarily always already "there for us." If I have to invent my projects utterly anew, what provides the context or relevance for me to get that project off the ground? We begin by implicitly accepting a pre-structured world. Certainly, our evolutionary history does a lot of that for us. When in doubt, what is relevant to eating, "dating", and fleeing things trying to eat me will give me definite concerns to think about!

Remember, however, human beings do our pre-cognitive sorting not just on biological terms but also culturally. Our ways of getting around and making sense of things, however much we might like to believe otherwise, presuppose complex social organizations. Aristotle was correct when he defined humanity not only as the rational but also the political (social) animal,

---

Disclosed: John Haugeland's Heidegger. Ed. Joseph Rouse. Cambridge, MA: Harvard University Press, 2013; and James Madden, *Thinking About Thinking: Mind and Meaning in the Age of Technological Nihilism* (Cascade, forthcoming).

and further claimed that an utterly solitary human would really be "either a wild beast or a god," either subhuman or superhuman.[13]

At the very least a fully cognitive human is linguistic, and language is an indisputably social affair. Thus, we always begin with something we have inherited from other people who were already up and running on the human project. Our first move is to fit in with what the others (mostly our elders and established authorities) have already laid down in terms of relevance and meaning. I didn't invent English, so I had to learn it to get along first and foremost. Thus, we would expect that very smart animals like us, who primarily get by through complex social organizations, will be deft conformers.

Evolutionary psychologist William von Hippel recounts a well-known experiment that bears this out. If you present human children and chimps with a box containing a treat and then show them a procedure for unlocking the box, both the chimps and the children will, after relatively few examples of the procedure, pick-up on the game and manage to open the box.

Now, if the scenario is varied, such that the box is transparent so as to reveal that some of steps in the procedure are unnecessary to opening the box, e.g., poking a stick into certain holes in the box clearly not connected to the locking mechanism, "the chimps modeled only the necessary actions and ignored the irrelevant ones, but the children continued to model the actions that were now obviously unnecessary."[14] Whereas the chimps were inclined to go their own way when it was obvious that the authority was putting them on, the human children tended to conform to the procedure as it was presented. So much for our radical individualism!

Likewise, comparative psychologist Michael Tomasello reports an array of experiments suggesting the human children will stick to their roles in games, even when it is obvious that they could obtain the motivating treat by circumventing the prescribed process, contrary to what we find in chimpanzees.[15] Again, for us it's not just getting what we want, but getting what we want together with other humans in a cooperative scheme. Cooperation, fulfilling previously prescribed roles, and conformity to authority are all seemingly baked into the human cake.

---

[13] Aristotle, *Politics*, trans. C.D.C. Reeve (Indianapolis, Indiana: Hackett Publishing, 2017), 1252a29. Aristotle thinks of rationality as linguistically expressed, and language is a social phenomenon. Thus, for him, our rational standing and our political (social) nature cannot be separated.

[14] William von Hippel, *The Social Leap: The New Evolutionary Science of Who We Are, Where We Come From, and What Makes us Happy* (New York: Harper Wave, 2018), p. 54.

[15] Michael Tomasello, *A Natural History of Human Thinking* (Cambridge, MA: Harvard, 2014), pp. 38-43.

All of this makes sense, when you consider how complex human cognition is, and how much sorting for relevance is involved. That is, the coming online of a human mind presupposes a great deal of transmission of *cultural knowledge* about *how we do things* and what is *relevant to us*. This presupposes that we are willing to listen and learn, and even conform when we don't quite get the plan or it runs contrary to some of our more direct interests. I don't want you to go on a radically individualist moment of self-definition while we are trying to negotiate a four-way stop in heavy traffic. I need to be able to expect that you'll conform to our prescribed roles, if I am going to cooperate too.

In short, we must be able to listen, learn, and conform, if we are going to maintain the sorts of complex social systems necessary for our distinctively human way of being in the world. As von Hippel puts it, "If I understand that another person has knowledge that I don't have, then I also understand that this person might impart knowledge on me. This understanding prompts me to pay close attention to potential teachers and to imitate their actions even if I don't discern their purpose."[16]

In other words, our tendency to social conformity is what makes the relationships of teaching and learning that are necessary for human cognition possible. Moreover, much of what we do as humans, probably most of what we do, is something we do with others to achieve common goals. Thus "a number of earlier adaptations for joint intentionality (e.g., joint goals, common conceptual ground, recursive inferences), and that its eventual emergence was part of a larger process in which human activities were conventionalized and normativized" were and are integral for our type of rationality to come online.[17] Our accepting and sticking to a socially prescribed role is an ineliminable element in distinctively human cognition.

Of course, our human tendency for conformity and role-playing is not all "upside," and the corresponding downside is very steep. You are probably aware of Stanley Milgram's famous experiments wherein he demonstrated that it is surprisingly easy to get people to do things that they thought were cruel when recognized authorities told them to do so.[18] There were some outliers who refused, and others conformed only while suffering

---

[16] Von Hipple, *The Social Leap*, p. 53.

[17] Tomasello, *A Natural History of Human Thinking*, p. 127.

[18] See Stanly Milgram, *Obedience to Authority: An Experimental View* (New York: Harper, 2009). Of course, Milgram's experiments from the 1950s are now fairly dated and controversial. For more recent psychological work that affirms the strong tendency to conform to authority, see Kathleen Taylor, *Brainwashing: The Science of Thought Control* (New York: Oxford University Press, 2017); and Mattias Desmett, *The Psychology of Totalitarianism* (White River Junction, VT: Chelsea Green Publishing, 2022).

great emotional consternation, but most subjects did what they were told to by authorities wearing white lab coats.

On the one hand, it is a great benefit that it is pretty easy to get lots of us onboard with a common project. The cliché is about the difficulty in "herding cats" not "herding humans." The latter is actually pretty easily done, and that has enabled humans to reach some amazing achievements. The Moon Shot and building the Great Pyramid required a lot of conformity and obedience. On the other hand, one of our chief weaknesses is that it is easy to get lots of us onboard with a common project, which is why it's not all that difficult to convince us to load our fellows onto trains making one-way trips to concentration camps.[19] Once again, there is a kind of double-edged sword right in the middle of the human cognitive toolbox. Get used to that irony.

Finally, our thinking is partly enabled by, and therefore partly limited by, our *technological extensions into our immediate environment.* What I have in mind here is a proposal now mainstream in contemporary cognitive science known as the "extended theory of mind" and the "embedded mind thesis." However you parse the details metaphysically, human cognition involves the translation of inscriptions in the central nervous system into conscious thoughts.

For example, at some level, Cormac's judgment that "Paris is the capital of France" involves his somehow recalling and combining information that was already encoded in his brain and calling that combination into explicit awareness. Does it matter, however, where that information was encoded before Cormac's judgment? Suppose he didn't have it memorized, but instead wrote it in his notebook for his geography class? Is there really any difference in principle as to whether Cormac's judgment is based on the living notes in his head or the dead notes in his notebook? Either way, he seems to have the same relation to the prior storage of the information.

Certainly, Cormac could lose the notebook, but he can also lose the notes in his head, e.g., a brain injury leading to memory loss. Either way, Cormac's relation to the means of thinking "Paris is the capital of France" are precarious, so there is no reason to say one is any more or less his or a part of his thinking. Where the information is stored has no bearing on whether it is intrinsic to Cormac's thinking.

Likewise, whether Cormac does his algebra problems entirely in his head or with the aid of a pencil and paper has no bearing on whether the answers are the results of his thinking. "Where" the calculation is done doesn't change any of that. In short, we have good reasons to conclude that our thinking does not exclusively go on in our heads, but can be extended into our

---

[19] See Christopher Browning, *Ordinary Men: Reserve Police Battalion 101 and the Final Solution in Poland* (New York: Harper, 2017). For a profound philosophical reflection on this issue, see Hannah Arendt, *Eichmann in Jerusalem: A Report on the Banality of Evil* (New York: Penguin, 2007).

equipment, e.g., notebooks, scratch paper, computers, cell phones, and even things like road signs.[20]

These are not merely incidental cases, but clues to one of the most distinctive aspects of human cognition: we are master "off-loaders" of our cognitive labor in our environment. Since we are linguistic and tool-making beings, we can develop all orders of devices (signs, written language, different types of clothing, etc.) that do a lot of our thinking for us. The exit sign spares me the need to find and remember the escape route just in case I need it. A wedding band helps to clarify the mating situation. My cell phone absolves me of all the trouble of remembering phone numbers and directions to the restaurant, etc., etc. Our works of art, social institutions, and long-standing human relationships provide for us an externalized source of information and cognition that far outstrips what we can do on our own.

This ability to off-load the burden of thinking and remembering is a great evolutionary advantage for our species, since we all have access to far more than what can be thought or remembered by any single animal. Other animals do this to some degree, but we are the masters (as far as we know). As the cognitive scientist Andy Clark puts it, "advanced cognition depends crucially on our ability to dissipate reasoning: to diffuse achieved knowledge and practical wisdom through complex structures, and to reduce the loads on individual brains by locating those brains in complex webs of linguistic, social, political and institutional constraints."[21] Clark sees our thinking as "parasitizing environmental resources" to such a degree that we need to abandon "the traditional boundaries between mind and the world themselves,"[22] and we should see that our *thinkings* and *doings* "are determined and explained by the intimate, complex, continued interplay between brain, body, and world" where "world" is partly the environment we have constructed for ourselves technologically.[23]

Note well that according to the extended mind thesis, we cannot really separate human cognition from human tool use. Our primary technological innovation is information technology, and that is as old as human thinking itself. As Clark and Chalmers put it in their classic paper:

---

[20] For a detailed and influential defense of the extended mind thesis, which I am parroting here, see Clark and Chalmers, "The Extended Mind," *Analysis* 58.1 (1998), pp. 7–19. See also Matthew Crawford's excellent book, *The World Beyond Your Head: On Becoming an Individual in an Age of Distraction* (New York: Farrar, Strauss, and Giroux, 2016), for an excellent introduction to the extended mind thesis.

[21] Clark, *Being There*, 180.

[22] Ibid., 62.

[23] Ibid. 217.

Moreover, it may be that the biological brain has in fact evolved and matured in ways which factor in the reliable presence of a manipulable external environment. It certainly seems that evolution has favored onboard capacities which are especially geared to parasitizing the local environment so as to reduce memory load, and even to transform the nature of the computational problems themselves . . . Perhaps there are other cases where evolution has found it advantageous to exploit the possibility of the environment being in the cognitive loop. If so, then external coupling is part of the truly basic package of cognitive resources that we bring to bear on the world . . . Once we recognize the crucial role of the environment in constraining the evolution and development of cognition, we see that extended cognition is a core cognitive process, not an add-on extra.[24]

All that is to say that human cognitive development is in a feedback loop with human technological development. Much of what has driven our thinking forward is our increased ability to manipulate our environment to bear our cognitive burdens, i.e., to off-load our thinking onto our information technology that structures our immediate locality—in fact, it is essential to the process.

Consider what a boon the ability to write simple notes is for working memory, one of the essential rudiments of distinctively human cognition. But what we can develop technologically is also determined by what we can already think. Human thinking is a product of the human environment, while the human environment is likewise, to some extent, a product of human thinking; the natural human environment is a world shaped by our information technology.

There is no pre-technological, Edenic state of human thought. These two have always gone hand-in-glove. Thus, once again, we can see that human cognition is both enabled and limited by our technological development. *What we can think* is in part enabled by what we are able to create in terms of information technology. Conversely, *what we cannot think* is likewise partly determined by the inadequacies of our creative means for rigging our environment cognitively. The extended mind gives us ground we can stand on, but in doing so it limits us in the territory we can cover.

You should have noticed a pattern in the foregoing discussion: all three aspects of human cognition we have discussed may take as much as they give. For example, our ability to sort our experiences and potential cognitions for relevance makes it possible for us to engage in coherent and workable thinking, but the very notion of "sorting" implies that we are leaving behind (in an unstated background or even off our "radar" entirely) more than we are

---

[24] Chalmers and Clark, "The Extended Mind," 31-32.

taking in. In order to have a practically useful take on things, we have to studiously (even if unconsciously) ignore most of what is "out there."

We can see this, too, in the social nature of our cognition. We must think as part of some community, and that makes all the social resources for cognition available to us. Nevertheless, *we* are then limited to what *we* can think, and that is, once again, likely just a small carve-out from a far larger and more complex reality. As we just saw, our information technology greatly enhances our ability to understand the world and deal with it practically, but our dependence on that very same technology likely leads us to leave much behind, unseen and unknown, because our tools simply are not apt to capture it.

Notice, too, that the histories of our relevance sorting, social organization, and technological development are all *contingent*. That is, the history of biological and cultural evolution came to prioritize things for us. The ways we have arranged ourselves socially, and what we have happened upon technologically *all could have gone very differently*. We are left then with the sneaking suspicion that there is much else to be known, but because of our contingent human circumstances, we are just not capable of getting to it.

Our relevance sorting, social organizations, and information tools get something right (I'm not calling that into question), but they do so by leaving as much out of the picture as they include. We have to admit that there are infinitely many other ways of framing reality that are likely just as good or, maybe, even better than ours. We're stuck with the one we just so happen to have, with nothing more to recommend it than that it's the only one we have.

It is important to emphasize that I am not suggesting a "brains in vats" or "simulation hypothesis" scenario according to which "it's all just in our heads." In fact, I think there are very good reasons to resist such views.[25] Rather, what we think about is really "out there," but it is something of a caricature of the full complexity (or chaos) of the fullness of being. It's not that the plant I perceive on my porch is just a figment of my mind, but that the way our minds work is such that we can only perceive that plant by ignoring a great many other things that might have been perceived by animals with different developmental histories and survival strategies.

Some of this ignorance is probably built into our cognitive hardware; we did not evolve to waste our psychological energies on things that are irrelevant to *our* well-being. Our thinking isn't illusory, it's just rigorously selective. We don't live in a dream, but a convenient simplification. The cost of having something definite to talk or think about is to leave a great share of things indefinite. This is not a problem that will be overcome by our gradual increase in knowledge, because anything we can learn will always be limited-enabled by these factors in our human cognitive toolbox. Every great

---

[25] See my *Thinking About Thinking*.

discovery in physics or insightful construction by a poet is operating within human limitations and will thus only be a partial take on reality. That, however, is the price of having a take on things at all.

We might think of this in terms of a *cave* as a metaphor and play on the fact that it seems many of our ancestors spent some time dwelling in caves. In fact, in this metaphorical sense, we are all still *cave-dwellers*. Human cognition works by and through carving out caves of relevance, social organization, and technological operation. We mine caves for ourselves, and those are the spaces of meaning and rationality we need in order to survive. Of course, the cave is real, and what goes on in it is important. Nevertheless, the caves we make for ourselves are convenient selections, caricatures of the fullness of reality.

We cannot help but to worry that these simplifications are all-too convenient and leave us ripe for manipulation and unwelcome surprise by things coming at us from our inherited and inevitable cognitive blind spots. Once again, it's our cave-dwelling status that makes us apt to send our fellows to camps, and we can only be confident that our modes of cognition have worked for the better given what we have encountered *so far*. Who knows what else is out there, previously irrelevant to our thinking, that might eventually run into us in uncanny ways; things that don't and can't make sense to us. These suspicions should lead us to a certain anxiety and humility once we have embraced our standing as cave-dwellers.

I'm sure many of you have noticed that my selection of *the cave* as a metaphor is not innocent, as it plays a role in one of the founding notions of Western philosophy. Plato famously used just such an analogy to explain his theory of education, or, better, philosophical enlightenment, in his canonical dialogue, *Republic*.

Plato has Socrates (the main character in his dialogue) offer a fable beginning with prisoners who have spent their entire lives chained in the cave, unable to see anything but shadows cast on the walls. One of the prisoners, and Plato famously does not explain why this guy is so lucky, frees himself and sees that the shadows are just images cast from figures being held up by other people. In short, the prisoner realizes that the cave is a caricature of reality, mostly a *put-on* by the social and technical situation he has been thrown into. He begins an arduous and unpleasant ascent out of the cave (He is being dragged, but by whom?), which represents the difficult and anxious process of enlightenment. It is uncomfortable to realize your lifeworld is a caricature.

Eventually, the liberated prisoner makes it out of the cave, but things are no more pleasant out there. The light hurts his eyes, as he was primarily reared to see in the dark. He can't stay long, and only can get glimpses of the Sun, the source of light. The newly minted philosopher, in this version of the tale, goes back in the cave to tell his fellows what they are missing. Of course, this is a hard sell: it's difficult to get there, it hurts to be there, and there is no way to talk about it when you come back in our mother tongue (the language of the cave). According to Plato's version of the tale, the philosopher persists in his efforts to save his friend, and as a result he risks execution by his fellow cave-dwellers.

This, no doubt, is a none-too-thinly veiled reference to Socrates' execution over his attempt to liberate his fellow Athenians from themselves after he realized that much of their common life was a sham. Socrates came to realize he and his fellow citizens were living in an all-too-convenient world they had made for themselves, and it was bringing their once great city to ruin. Certainly, the powers that be (those people putting on the shadowy puppet show on the walls) would prefer to keep things nice and cozy in the cave, but it's not all maniacal conspiracy (though I think Plato thinks some of it is!).[26]

Human nature itself is ordered to cave-dwelling. We need our ordinary everyday humdrum "certainties." We cannot stand very long outside the cave; we need to live by caricatures. Thus, even the most enlightened soul will sooner or later succumb to the temptation to conform to the conveniences of the cave. Any insight we get about what is outside our cave, sooner or later, will be lost almost entirely in our attempts to make sense of it in the language of us cave-dwellers.

That is The Problem: the conditions of our ordinary human existence impose on us a kind of ignorance about what is beyond our everyday world, and there are dangers in settling for that ignorance, but it is hard to see how we can ever get past our dependence on the very conditions that bind us to this ignorance.

Indeed, Plato has Socrates in several places in his dialogues (e.g., *Phaedo*) claim that enlightenment can come only after a certain kind of *death*. Living outside the cave is not a sustainable human possibility, so it requires being "dead to the world," if not literally a post-mortem existence. Nevertheless, Plato has his version of Socrates face this death with unflinching bravery, because it is possibly an occasion for liberation from the conditions of human ignorance. We can't just give ourselves over to our self-imposed ignorance. I believe the following remarks make Plato's point perfectly:

> The struggle of the soul to come into its own autonomous existence
> is a struggle against unexamined presuppositions, the unexamined

---

[26] By the time Plato wrote *Republic*, the main characters of the dialogue were deceased, and most of them died in the violent political tit-for-tat that followed Athens' defeat in the Peloponnesian War, including Plato's own brothers, Glaucon and Adeimantus. Plato had no doubts about the fact that dangerous powers do indeed work very hard to maintain certain aspects of the cave. See Martha Nussbaum, *The Fragility of Goodness: Luck and Ethics in Greek Tragedy and Ethics* (Cambridge: Cambridge University Press, 2001).

life, taking things for granted. The body is not the prison of the soul; on the contrary, the prison is constituted by secondhand knowledge, idle talk, average everydayness, mediocrity. The prison is inauthenticity. The soul of the philosopher needs to be dead to what 'they' say, needs to release itself from thralldom to the ways things are bandied about in everyday chatter. The soul comes into its own by separating itself from everyday life. That, if we read Plato carefully, is how philosophizing is dying. In other words, the Socratic method, refusal to accept the usual substitution of beings for Being, coincides with philosophizing, with separating the soul from its prison, with authentic anticipation of death.[27]

Plato's message for us regarding our ironic intertwining of cognitive limitation and enablement is itself a mix of hope and pessimism: the truth is out there, as it were, beyond our cave, but it seems that it would take a *superhuman* act to grasp it.[28] Nevertheless, this superhuman perspective is something that is demanded of us by our call to live authentically, i.e., to make the attempt to see beyond the bounds of our self-imposed ignorance.

There is a paradoxical nature to Plato's invitation to transcend the cave. He is asking us to outthink the very grounds of our thinking. If the cave (our biological/cultural sorting, social institutions, and technological developments) are the necessary conditions for our understanding anything at all, then how it is we can possibly go beyond the ignorance they impose on us.

As I have mentioned, this would be an act of superhuman (or at least non-human) cognition, but we are, obviously, all-too-human for any of that! Remember, things don't end well for Plato's liberated prisoner. We are *living humans*, and there is no getting around that as long as we draw breath! It seems then that another power from the outside would have to show up for us and impose itself on us. *Somebody* or *something* liberates the "lucky" prisoner and drags him through the unpleasant educational process of getting out of the cave.

That is all well and good, but what is to be done while we sit and wait for liberation? For Plato, we can only get a sense of what is outside the cave through a sort of memory or recollection. He argues that we get little reminders within our ordinary experience that we have our one foot in something greater than what goes on in our cave. We occasionally run across

---

[27] Richard Rojcewicz, *Heidegger, Plato, Philosophy, Death: An Atmosphere of Mortality* (New York: Rowman and Littlefield, 2021), p. 24.

[28] Yes, I am indeed playing on Jeff Kripal's use of "superhuman" in his *Superhumanities: Historical Precedents, Moral Objections, and New Realities* (Chicago: University of Chicago Press, 2022). I will have more to say about all of that in the following chapters.

hints that there is a much broader insight to be had, but all we have in this life are fleeting *memories* of another place we seem to have once been, or maybe we've always really been *there*, though we don't yet have eyes to see it.

After several hundred pages of arguing that there is a world beyond the cave and being frustratingly cagey as to what that greater reality is, Plato ends his *Republic* by having Socrates tell us a myth. In this tale, Er is an admirably virtuous man killed in battle. He, along with everyone else who has died, go to Hades where they are given opportunities to choose their reincarnated lives back in the world of the living. On their way back to the world (our world of the cave), Socrates claims:

> They camped, since evening was coming on, beside the river of forgetfulness, whose water no vessel can hold. All of them had to drink a certain measure of this water. But those not saved by wisdom drank more than the measure. And as each of them drank, he forgot everything.[29]

Er, who had achieved some wisdom in his immediate prior life, did not drink this water of forgetfulness, so he *remembers* where he was when he was dead. Plato's point is that some of us, the Er-types among us, have glimpses of where we all have been, or maybe always are, but these are just like memories now. Our only sense of what is outside the cave is a kind of memory, much as one recollects a dream she had the night before. Of course, such recollection is always subject to the basic distortions of human thinking, but these hints are all we get for now.[30]

So, what does any of this have to do with the UFO question? Consider one of the many fascinating and uncanny cases Whitley Strieber presents from his vast correspondence in *Them*. The case I have in mind was relayed by two people, one of whom is a perceptual psychologist, who independently contacted Strieber after he came out with his own contact

---

[29] Plato, *Republic*, trans C.D.C. Reeve (Indianapolis, IN: Hackett, 2004), pp. 325-326.

[30] I have dealt painfully quickly with Plato! I provide a much more detailed reading of the cave in my essay "Philosophy and Locality, Pt. 2: Socratic Piety" (https://jdmadden.substack.com/p/philosophy-and-locality-pt-2-socratic). You can also find a detailed discussion of the cave (as part of a complete course on Plato's Republic) on *Philosophy for the People* (https://www.youtube.com/watch?v=AWhT-i1Pts0&list=PL6T1Pj98hD6O2 4VL0dJH0nJgMSUsxD02M&index=7&t=294s). Finally, I make many of these connections with the UFO phenomenon in my conversation with Kelly Chase on *The UFO Rabbit Hole Podcast* (https://youtu.be/DgJt4vlOZjY).

experience. Strieber counts this case as "one of the strangest experiences I have ever come across," which is no small claim coming from him![31]

What the two witnesses saw (and since there are two of them and they made their reports independently, there is every reason to take their testimony seriously) really is beyond merely strange. They encountered a giant jet airliner, though it wasn't entirely like any conventional airplane, flying dangerously close to a freeway in Long Island (they thought it was going to crash into them), a billboard that eventually takes off as if it were some sort of alien craft, and a cadre of unsettling clowns and other sundry carnivalesque characters engaged in truly distressing and outright threatening behavior. All of this is the stuff of nightmares, and they both soberly claim to have seen these things (though, of course, they have slightly different perspectives), and remember that one of the witnesses is an academic expert on distinguishing veridical perception from hallucination.

The *content* of their experience is curious enough, but the uncanniest thing about it is its *context*: these events occurred on a busy freeway, but only these two witnesses (as far as we know) saw any of these distressing phenomena. You would think a plane nearly crashing into a busy highway interchange, the launching of a billboard into the sky, and the insidious presence of a circus of threatening characters would have made the news, but we only have these two men to attest to the event.

Maybe we have some tools to make sense of that odd fact. The other drivers on that Long Island freeway, just like the rest of us, were taken in by the images on the walls of the cave of their everyday existence. Whatever is behind these strange phenomena, it wasn't relevant to their "world," and it certainly isn't something recognized as such by the social arrangements that structure their thinking. Strieber himself applies some of the psychological literature suggesting our powerful ability to dissociate from or ignore obvious phenomena when they don't fit into our practical tasks or preferred concerns. Likely, the vast majority of us would keep ourselves safely in the cave in this situation, which raises the unsettling question of what is going on outside my window right now that I'm missing because I'm too comfortable in the ordinary, and practically necessary, state of human ignorance.

If almost everybody on that freeway missed the giant airplane and the menacing clowns, then it's quite plausible that we are all ignorant of a vastly more complicated set of beings and goings-on constantly surrounding us. This, as we have discussed, is simply how human cognition works; we simplify so as to render things manageable, but simplification always leaves something out. Strieber's accounts in *Them.* strongly suggest that we are missing out on quite a lot, except in those rare and mysterious cases of experiencers who

---

[31] Strieber, *Them.*, p. 11.

seem to be privileged (or cursed) with a glimpse of what is outside our common cave.

He also shows us how, like Plato's liberated prisoner, this enlightenment often comes at a dear price, not the least of which is scorn from those of us still exclusively oriented to life in the cave. The cost of seeing something beyond our everyday caricature of things, at least if one is honest about it, is obscurity and persecution among one's fellow cave-dwellers.

The disapprobation by our peers and domineering authorities is not the only downside to enlightenment: realizing that our "world" is not the full story, that things are far more complex and unmanageable than we would like to (or need to) think is certainly a source of dire anxiety, especially for those who have seen something from "out there" face-to-face. There must be a sneaking sense of a sort of death, the demise of our comfortable world of everydayness. In short, we should see Strieber's work and the experience of many of the people who report encounters as real-life iterations of Plato's archetypical allegory. We are witnessing the playing out of a fundamental structure of human existence.

It is interesting to consider that Strieber's correspondents tell their stories using items drawn from common experience, which are at the same time a bit off. For example, the airplane is much like an ordinary commercial jet, but there's also much that is strange about it; the clowns are much like conventional circus characters, and yet they don't really fit that description comfortably.[32] Etc., etc. There is also the question of why "aliens" (and, as you shall see, I'm not one to privilege the Extraterrestrial Hypothesis) would show up in airplanes or dressed up like clowns.

Moreover, as it is often pointed out, why would they even be quasi-humanoid at all? These phenomena are all too close to *our* ordinary experience. Too good to be true similarities with ordinary experience could recommend hallucination or elaborate hoaxes, but in many of these cases I don't think that is the most plausible explanation. Rather, maybe even our experiencers are subconsciously trying to put these encounters from beyond the cave into cave-dwelling categories. We simply have nothing else to go on. Our only tools for interpreting our experiences come from the resources ready-at-hand in the cave. As I said above, all attempts to articulate experiences beyond the cave (even our attempts to articulate them to ourselves) are doomed to be rendered just one more caricature of a far more complex and inarticulable reality in the words and categories that work within our necessary human limitations.

---

[32] John Keel's detailed account of various mysterious airplane flaps in the first half of the twentieth century in *Operation Trojan Horse* (New York: Putnam, 1970) are particularly instructive on this point.

Thus, anytime we find ourselves speaking of something seemingly from outside our caves, whatever completes the sentence "It was like a . . ." will likely render the statement false. These experiences are mostly unlike anything we are designed to deal with. An attempt to describe something for which you have no analogy in our ordinary cognitive toolbox will end in a silly caricature. There will just be various ways of getting it wrong.

If we are going to start on the path of making some sense of the UFO phenomenon (supposing that is a path we can even begin to travel), *we must discipline ourselves against being too quick to trust any of our intuitions about what we are encountering.* What we are getting from our attempts to describe these encounters are as much expressions of our own presuppositions, self-images, and human limitations (and likely manipulations of these human limitations by those among us particularly interested in maintaining a nicely managed cave) as they are accurate depictions of what triggered the events. There may be no final and complete way of teasing out what in the experience is really there from what is the product of how we happen to think about things. Strieber makes much the same point here:

> This is typical of the sort of contradiction that is inherent to contact. If they are from within our world in some way that, perhaps because of how we perceive and think, we cannot understand clearly, then what we are looking at here is a sort of mirror, but one that is balanced on a strange shadow-line between mind and matter.[33]

Strieber is correct to push the consequences of these insights to the point of questioning some of the most fundamental dichotomies by which our thinking is structured, e.g., mind vs. matter, and in what follows I will argue that taking the UFO seriously should lead us to see that a lot of our most cherished distinctions have a far more limited application than we typically think.[34]

The primary lesson of the UFO is humility. We don't know nearly as much as we think we do, and we might not be set up cognitively to do much better. Thus, I doubt *what* Strieber's correspondents saw were clowns and an airplane, though they certainly saw those objects as just *that*. But that is no strike against their truthfulness. What they saw was really there, and they saw it (or subconsciously interpreted their vision) in the ways they report. The

---

[33] Strieber, *Them.*, p. 7

[34] None of this is anything terribly innovative on either Strieber's or my part. Carl Jung already saw the UFO phenomenon as supportive of his prior questioning of the mind-matter dichotomy and he cautions us against mistaking our interpretive scheme with the intrinsic nature of what is behind appearances in his classic treatment of the issue in *Flying Saucers: A Modern Myth of Things Seen in the Sky* (Princeton, NJ: Princeton University Press, 1979).

origin of that experience was something poking its head in from outside our cave, so there is as much error as truth in any human description of such phenomena, though that's to some degree true of all human experiences.

I find the following remarks from Strieber very helpful:

> . . . are we dealing not with rare experiences at all but rather a common one that is rarely remembered? . . . Because of the distortions that are fundamental to this whole story, it is going to be impossible to answer a question like that definitively.[35]

> Are encounters actually not "alien" contact at all, but an unknown part of nature and of what it is to be human? If so, then perhaps what is rare is not encounters like this but recall of them.[36]

The picture I have painted so far suggests that the UFO phenomenon is not necessarily "alien," but something that has always been with us, just outside the entrance to our cave, and this is a theme I will pursue in detail throughout the rest of this book. Maybe it is something that we have been running into unawares for our entire history, like the hapless drivers on that Long Island freeway missing out on the utterly displacing scene unfolding all around them as they hurriedly drive home in time for dinner.

In the passages I quote above, Strieber invokes the notion of recollection and memory as central to the contact experience. For that reason, we might think of the contactee as much like Plato's resurrected hero, Er: that rare (or maybe not so rare) human being who has come back from "death" with some, however vague and distorted, *memory* of what was out there beyond the limitations of ordinary human life. For Strieber, no less than for Plato, the world of the dead might be the real world.

The following well-known remarks from William James articulate these ideas well:

> We may be in the universe as dogs and cats in our libraries, seeing the books and hearing the conversation, but having no inkling of the meaning of it all.[37]

> I believe, rather, that we stand in much the same relation to the whole of the universe as our canine and feline pets do to the whole of human life. They inhabit our drawing-rooms and libraries. They take

---

[35] Strieber, *Them.*, p. 42

[36] Ibid., p. 45.

[37] William James, *A Pluralistic Universe*, in *Writings: 1902-1910* (New York: Literary Classics of the United States, 1987), p. 771.

part in the scenes of whose significance they have no inkling. They are merely tangent to curves of history, the beginnings and ends and forms of which pass wholly beyond their ken. So we are tangent to the wider life of things. But, just as many of the dog's and cat's ideals coincide with our ideals, and dogs and cats have daily living proof of that fact, so we may well believe, on the proofs that religious experience affords, that higher powers exist and are at work to save the world on ideal lines similar to our own.[38]

James takes "religious experience," i.e., encounters with the truly uncanny, to be evidence that we are denizens of a world that far outstrips our ken—we are like dogs and cats in a library or a living room full of humans in a deep conversation. The dogs and cats get only inchoate glimpses of this broader world that is not what they are designed to comprehend, the proverbial vision through the glass darkly. What the dogs and cats see and hear is limited by the very conditions of their distinctively dog and cat perception and cognition, and this leaves behind vast swaths of what is really going on.

Do dogs and cats understand that we are the ones really running things in the library or the drawing-room? Whatever we might think about James' optimism regarding the workings of these beings that exist outside our particular animal cave, the important point to take away is that *our position in this analogy is not the humans, but the dogs and cats.* The encounter with the uncanny, including the sorts of experiences Streiber recounts, is evidence against our comforting humanistic pretensions. Though some of us overhear the conversations of the superhumans in the vicinity, most of us blithely go about mundane matters without noticing any of the suggestions of a richer world just outside the cave.

That vast library or drawing-room, inhabited by much more sophisticated intelligences, goes about its far more complex business quite well without our attention. In fact, these encounters from the edge of our cognitive limitations show that we are not in fact running things in this world (we're the pets) and we might not even understand some of the events in which we participate: "Our dogs . . . are in our human life but not of it. They witness hourly the outward body of events whose inner meaning cannot, by any possible operation, be revealed to their intelligence—events in which they themselves often play the cardinal part."[39] The point of the whole show might not be us after all, but Them.

---

[38] William James, *Pragmatism*, in *Writings: 1902-1910*, p. 619.

[39] William James, *The Will to Believe and Other Popular Essays*, in *Writings: 1878-1899* (New York: Literary Classics of the United States, 1992), p. 499.

2 Aristotle, Myth, and Extraterrestrial Intelligences: An Ancient "Super Natural" Philosophy of Religion

"If we followed in [Aristotle's] footsteps, drawing on our sciences, from theoretical physics to engineering, economics and ethics, what conclusions would we reach? If we are to be Aristotelians now it cannot be by parroting Aristotle's theories. Instead, it must be by taking him as a paradigm of how we might be philosophers and theologians ourselves—a 'paradigm in the heavens,' so to speak, 'for anyone who wishes to look at it and to found himself on the basis of what he sees.'" (Plato, Republic 529b).

—C.D.C. Reeve, *Introduction* to *Aristotle's Theology: The Primary Texts*[40]

"It is a sure sign of the death of a religion when its mythic presuppositions become systematized, under the severe rational eyes of an orthodox rationalism, into a ready sum of historical events, and when people begin timidly defending the veracity of myth but at the same time resisting its natural continuance—when the feeling for myth withers and its place is taken by a religion claiming historical foundations."

—Nietzsche, *The Birth of Tragedy*, §X[41]

"If these things are real—and by all human standards it hardly seems possible to doubt this any longer—then we are left with only two hypotheses: that of

---

[40] C.D.C. Reeve. (ed. and trans), *Aristotle's Theology: The Primary Texts* (Indianapolis, IN: Hackett Publishing) 2023), p. xlvii.

[41] Friedrich Nietzsche, *The Birth of Tragedy*, trans Francis Goffling (New York: Anchor Books, 1956), p. 68.

their weightlessness on the one hand and of their psychic nature on the other. This is a question I, for one, cannot decide."

— C.G. Jung, *Flying Saucers: A Modern Myth of Things Seen in the Skies*[42]

"Both the technological and fictional readings of something like the UFO phenomenon are part of the same world-story . . . materialism. On one level, materialism is just more monotheism in disguise. It is another jealous god. Instead of 'My God is the only God,' now it is 'There is only matter.' The story goes like this. Matter is made up of tiny dead things that are bouncing or waving around in predictable mathematical patterns. It's all math. There is no meaning. There is no mind. Evolution is without a goal. It intends nothing. It is going nowhere. The universe is pointless."

— Jeffrey Kripal, *The Super Natural: Why the Unexplained in Real*[43]

Aristotle's natural theology is a complicated and controversial affair. The upshot is that he arrives at the conclusion that there must be a system of eternal moving movers (*the gods* in the heavens) explanatorily united by a single unmoved mover (*the god, out beyond the first or primary heaven*). Note well that Aristotle claims to arrive at the existence of *the gods* and *the god scientifically*, i.e. by making deductive inferences based on requirements for the intelligibility of empirical phenomena.

Basically, he is impressed by the fact that sublunary substances, i.e., earthly beings composed of the basic elements (earth, air, water, and fire) move eternally. That is, terrestrial beings have come to be and passed away forever (and will do so forever). By Aristotle's light, such motion (the coming to be and passing away of beings composed of earth, air, water and/or fire) cannot account for itself (even if it is eternal), so it must be accounted for by a higher-order intelligibility that pulls all this earthly motion into a coherent system of change.

This cause of motion moves concretely existing beings, so it must be a concrete thing. This mover of earthly things cannot be moved in the same way, otherwise we have only kicked the can down the explanatory road; we are trying to explain earthly motion, but Aristotle believes that requires something super-earthly to do the work. That is, the mover of earthly substances must

---

[42] C.G. *Jung, Flying Saucers: A Modern Myth of Things Seen in the Skies*, trans. R.F.C. Hull (Princeton, N.J.: Princeton University Press, 1978), p.109.

[43] Whitley Strieber and Jeffrey Kripal, *The Super Natural: Why the Unexplained is Real* (New York: Tarcher Perigee, 2016), p. 309.

be *unmoved* relative to earthly substances, i.e., it cannot be moved by them nor can it be moved in the same way. The higher-order mover is utterly *independent* with respect to earthly movers. Since earthly motion is eternal (infinite into both the past and the future), the higher-order mover must then be *eternal*. Moreover, this higher-order mover, since it accounts for earthly movement cannot be composed of the earthly elements (earth, air, water, and fire), and it is therefore *immaterial* with respect to earthly beings.

The mode of causality by which this relatively unmoved/immaterial mover moves earthly beings is curious, since it must cause motion in earthly beings without being in earthly motion (otherwise it would fail as an explanation of such motion). The higher-order mover of earthly motion does not intervene in earthly affairs. Earthly beings must be moved by an *attraction* to this relatively unmoved/immaterial mover (desire, contemplation, or some such).

Suppose the moon, for instance, is the higher-order mover of earthly movers. The moon is then *eternal* (immortal), relatively *immaterial* (it's not made of earthly elements), *unmoving, aloof,* and *independent* to the earthly beings it moves by its intrinsic *attractiveness (nobility, goodness).* That is to say, for Aristotle, the moon is a deity. Notice, however, the recurring qualifier, "relatively," that needs to be appended to this higher-order mover. The moon is immaterial, invariant, independent, etc. *relative to earthly beings, but it still moves.*

Thus, there must be a higher-order of intelligibility that moves the moon by some sort of attraction and so on. The moon is likewise a relatively lower-order being whose motion is accounted for by its attraction to a relatively higher-order deity that is independent, immaterial, and unmoving with respect to it, say, Mercury. Even Mercury is also a relatively unmoved mover, so it too must serve a yet higher-order deity.

This recursion of intelligibility, according to Aristotle, cannot go on to infinity, and therefore, there must be a final heaven that synthesizes all of these hierarchies of deities (eternal movers) into an astronomical system. Such a heaven would be a first-moving mover, so there must be something that moves it, which is moved by nothing else. For Aristotle, to be moved by nothing else is to be not moved at all. Thus, *the god*, the storied unmoved mover, contemplates only itself (it is attracted only to itself), while moving everything else solely by its irresistible attractiveness. The god is unqualifiedly unmoving, immaterial, and independent.

Notice that the principle moving the system is not physical momentum *à la* Newtonian physics, but desire or attraction. Aristotle's cosmology entails a universe suffused with beings whose motion is explained by a cognitive or quasi-cognitive relation to the beings that stand over them in terms of intelligibility (higher-order divinities). We might say that *Aristotle's universe runs on worship* or *interlocking hierarchies of contemplative admiration.*

Each level of the universe looks up to a higher-order intelligence that gives intelligibility (either directly or by transitivity) to all cosmological levels below it, terminating in the being, the god, whose contemplative worthiness makes sense of the entire cosmological system. Aristotle is quite comfortable with the notion of extraterrestrial intelligences! For him, the extraterrestrials have always been running things.

That is all very quick, and there is plenty to be said in terms of critical reply (especially with respect to my paltry presentation of Aristotle's position), but my point in bringing Aristotle's natural theology up is not to take up the argumentation in detail, but to consider the status natural theology holds in Aristotle's systematic thinking. My main question is whether Aristotle's attempted demonstration of divinity is a proof of the *supernatural*. Or does Aristotle offer a sort of naturalistic reduction of the supernatural to tamer scientific categories?

On the one hand, Aristotle would have nothing to do with contemporary forms of naturalism that frequently (though not exclusively) argue that the "whole show," as C.S. Lewis famously puts it, can be accounted for in terms of the basic entities posited by contemporary physics. Aristotle is certainly no physical reductionist, and he is very critical of the Democritean atomism abroad in his day. We need to be careful here, too, as not all self-avowed naturalists are strict reductionists, but, in any event, the fact that Aristotle's biological and psychological treatises operate by explanatory categories to some degree autonomous with respect to his physics (e.g., he introduces the notion of soul in *De Anima* to capture what is unaccounted by substantial form in the *Physics*) is enough to show that Aristotle is nothing like what we might have in mind as a naturalist today. Moreover, remember Aristotle's universe runs on a sort of quasi-cognitive attractiveness between cosmological levels. That's not a picture of the world that sits well with most versions of contemporary naturalism.

On the other hand, there is a sense that Aristotle denies that there need be any supernatural explanation in our understanding of the movement of natural bodies. Aristotle's nature is free-standing; it requires no outside explanation. The gods and the god are not interveners from the outside of nature, but, in some sense, part of the system of nature. Nor are the gods or the god creators of the cosmological system. The universe, for Aristotle, has necessarily been up and running for an infinity, and it will continue for an infinity. Aristotle identifies the gods with the celestial bodies (planets and stars), and the god is the ultimate explanation of their motion, but the "whole show" can be explained within the categories of Aristotle's science (even though that explanatory system is richly pluralistic).

For Aristotle, *nature* is quite *super*, so there is no need for any notion of a *supernatural*. The super standing of nature is captured by a completed (metaphysical) science, and there is then no incongruity between a natural and a "supernatural" explanation. This leaves little room for a natural-supernatural distinction. Though he arrives at a metaphysics and cosmology that takes the universe as an interlocking hierarchy of divinely governed realms of intelligibility, Aristotle's story is entirely scientific and natural. These divinities, including the ultimate divinity, do not interrupt or intervene in nature, but instead are the completing principles of the intelligibility of nature. Aristotle's natural theology does not compete with his natural science, but brings it to its ultimate point of completion. All of this is to say that I don't think Aristotle's cosmology and metaphysics fits at all comfortably in any of the standard camps entrenched in contemporary debates, and this, for my money, is one of the virtues of his position (and I would say much the same regarding his approach to the soul).

Does this mean that Aristotle's cosmology is a sort of scientism, even if it is not narrowly naturalistic? Moreover, once we have incorporated divinity into our rational cosmology, what then of religion? That is, Aristotle's cosmology, though not naturalistic in terms of the sterile categories of contemporary philosophy, does offer an alternative explanation to the traditional mythological accounts covering some of the same ground. Aristotle thinks Mars is an intelligent divinity, but it's not at all clear that he has anything (or anyone) in the least like the Ares of traditional Greek mythology in mind.

Should we take Aristotle as debunking the traditional mythological religions? Having just finished outlining his metaphysical cosmology *cum* natural theology, Aristotle takes up the issue of popular religion explicitly:

> There is a tradition handed down from the ancients of the earliest times and bequeathed to posterity in the shape of a myth to the effect that the heavenly bodies are gods and that the divine encompasses the whole of nature. The rest of the tradition has been added later in a mythical way with a view to the persuasion of ordinary people and the view to its use for legal purposes and for what is advantageous. For they say these gods are human in form or like some of the other animals, and also other features similar that follow from or are similar to those just mentioned. But if we separate the first point from these additions and grasp it alone, namely, that they thought that the primary substances were gods, we would have to regard it as divinely said, and that while it is likely that each craft and each philosophy has often been developed as far as possible only to pass away again, these beliefs about the gods have survived like remnants until the present.

In any case, the belief of our forefathers and of our earliest predecessors is to this extent alone illuminating to us.[44]

This passage contains some of the most interesting and, for my money, under-appreciated things Aristotle claims. There are three types of epistemic relations to the gods that Aristotle considers.

First, there is an original or *Ur* insight, given in the form of some sort of myth, "to the effect that the heavenly bodies are gods and that the divine encompasses the whole of nature," and Aristotle has a high view for this "divinely said" mythos. It seems that our primordial ancestors had some deep insight or revelation regarding the relation of divinity to nature, even if they had no proper scientific understanding of these issues.

Second, there is a further elaboration of the primordial insight in terms of anthropomorphic and crassly animistic legends. Here, Aristotle seems to be mistrustful, chalking these elaborations up to legal and political techniques for persuading the populous. Aristotle, like his famous mentor (Plato) is attuned to the fact that we build caves for ourselves, and this process is subject to manipulation and control by those with the power to direct which shadows are cast on the way.

Finally, Aristotle has his own scientific account of divinity. What is interesting is that he seems to think that the original Ur mythos and his cutting-edge scientific demonstration arrive at essentially the same cosmological/theological conclusions. That is, he encourages us to separate the original mythical insight from its later politicized elaborations so that we can see that our primordial forefathers fundamentally agreed with his scientific findings, i.e., "the primary substances were gods." Aristotle is not above some bit of demythologizing, as he is happy to let the easily manipulated superhero stories pass away like all outmoded crafts and philosophies, but his de-mythological project is not totalizing. Aristotle concedes that "the belief of our forefathers and of our earliest predecessors is to this extent alone illuminating to us," i.e., to the extent that we leave behind the later elaborations, the original Ur myths are insightful and have something to teach us. Aristotle is open to the possibility that his distant ancestors had insights taking them beyond the cave, no less than he is confident that his own natural theology takes him "out there."

---

[44] Aristotle, *Metaphysics*, trans. Reeve (Indianapolis, IN: Hackett, 2016), 1074a36-1074b13). Reeve's introduction to the *Metaphysics* is a great source for further commentary on the issues I have introduced above, as is his introduction to *Aristotle's Theology*. See comprehensive introductions to Aristotle's thought, see Reeve's *Aristotle: A Quick Emersion* (New York: Tibidabo Publishing, 2019) and Jonathan Lear, *Aristotle: The Desire to Understand* (New York: Cambridge, 1988).

What I find fascinating here is that the "us" Aristotle is referring to seems to be those of us who have gone through the process of completing his cosmological science. In other words, the originary myths Aristotle has in mind (and he tantalizing does not give us a hint about them beyond their barest content) have something illuminating to say even to the student of First Philosophy. That is, Aristotle's rational cosmology purports to demonstrate divinity as suffusing nature and gets us over facile comic book caricatures of the divine, but it does not have all there is to say about the matter.

Even completed science can still be illuminated by the Ur myths. Thus, for Aristotle, it is not a question of science replacing mythology, nor does myth place some artificial limit on science. Rather, he seems to have a cross-germinating relationship in mind: on the one hand, science moves us to rational footing with respect to divinity while disabusing us of easily manipulated *faux* understandings, and on the other hand, the originary myths still provide some sort of insight that illuminates even scientific understanding. Science completes the picture in an explanatory sense (though in a way that includes divinity), but there is still something more to be said (or maybe shown) by the mythologized experiences of our primordial ancestors. There is a sort of insight or experience that is even super scientific, meta-metaphysical.

What exactly are these original insights or experiences that Aristotle claims have been passed down by our primordial ancestors? I don't know, but I think Jeffrey Kripal is trying very hard to find out. In fact, his method of investigation is something of a contemporary case of the methodological stance that Aristotle is suggesting in the passage I quoted above. Kripal is an expert in the comparative study of religion, a well-established academic, who takes very seriously all orders of paranormal phenomena that are typically dismissed out of hand in polite scholarly circles (unless of course something spooky happens to fit our preferred ideological or religious commitments). Here is how he describes the sorts of events he considers in a book he co-authored with Whitley Strieber:

> I collect and compare the earlier building blocks, the anomalous events or extraordinary experiences that may (or may not) eventually lead to a religious belief or institution. These anomalous building blocks, these tiny personal religions before religion, are historical facts, as real and as important as any other recurring historical fact. They *happen*. What they are actually *are* is quite another matter. But here is the thing. If you resist the temptation to believe these events (that is, provide them with some definite religious category, judgment, or interpretation) but instead collect them, arrange them into patterns, and put them on a flat, fair table to analyze, they remain "super" enough. But they no longer appear so odd, and they are certainly "anecdotal," as the debunkers like to label them (as if that

intellectual cop-out explains anything at all). Quite the opposite, these super states begin to look like universal, if always morphing attributes of a shared human mindspace. They begin to look, well, *natural*.[45]

Kripal shares Aristotle's view that the world does not fit at all neatly into the tired oppositional categories of contemporary academic debate, i.e., natural vs. supernatural, physical vs. non-physical, etc. Rather, Kripal suspects that anomalous phenomena (encounters with UFOs, apparitions, trance states, ESP, etc.) are not supernatural interventions into nature, but instead reveal that *nature is super*. That is, once we have done the careful phenomenological and hermeneutical work of collecting and analyzing these experiences, both in the distant past and among our contemporaries, we will find that they are too common and too well-patterned to dismiss.

The so-called anomalous is only anomalous to the degree that these occurrences are not welcome in some iteration of the consensus version of reality. Once we have committed to take experience seriously (including phenomena we don't much like taking seriously), then we will see that nature is pretty spooky. That's not because nature is full of gaps and miracles marking supernatural interventions, but because nature is quite super all on its own. "The heavenly bodies are gods" and "the divine encompasses the whole of nature," as Aristotle puts it. This is why Kripal and Strieber titled their book "The Super Natural" instead of "The Supernatural." Of course Kripal and Strieber are not out to defend Aristotelian cosmology (that's not the point), but they do operate by a view of the metaphysical standing of nature and divinity (the "super") interestingly akin to Aristotle's

There is also an important methodological commonality in this vicinity. One of Kripal's central methodological commitments is to steer a careful path between two common errors: *reductive comparison* and *religious comparison*. The former

> can be pictured as a straight arrow moving from right to left, that is, from a present worldview to a past one. Religious comparison can be thought of as an equally straight arrow moving from the left to the right, that is, from a past worldview to a present one. As the reversed arrow suggests, these two comparative practices are really not so different from each other. Which is another way of saying that they make the same mistake, if in opposite directions.[46]

---

[45] Kripal, *The Super Natural*, p. 6. Author's emphasis.
[46] Kripal, *The Super Natural*, p. 13.

In other words, reductive comparison pretends to a wholesale debunking of prior mythos (or contemporary myths like UFOs) as mistaken or obsolete primitive explanations that can now be superseded by rational and scientific understandings, e.g., "What the primitive Greeks thought were deities, we now know *just* to be planets." Religious comparisons make the opposite but analogous move of seeing rational and scientific findings or even recent "anomalous" experiences as truncated versions of a preferred religious mythology, e.g., "The planets are *just* a new way of talking about the gods like Mars" or "UFOs are angels and demons."

Instead of falling into either of these approaches (a choice between a tyranny of the past or a tyranny of the present), Kripal would have us take the experiences seriously, and ask what these basic encounters, once we have done the necessary phenomenological archeology that brackets both our contemporary (scientific) and religious expectations, show us about what nature is really like. This approach is again much like what Aristotle exhibits above. On the one hand, Aristotle does not take the popular mythological inheritance abroad in his day at face value. He believes his scientific findings give him ample grounds to set aside these anthropomorphic and animistic images that have been conveniently incorporated into our cave-dwelling caricature of the world. On the other hand, Aristotle is open to what a deep sort of "myth," or a primordial experience had by his distant forbearers, might be able to do in terms of illuminating his rational cosmology. Like Kripal, Aristotle (ever the empiricist!) recommends that we take experience seriously enough to bracket the complacency following on our scientific successes and the comfort of the preferred mythologies of our cultural moment.

Kripal and Aristotle are both open to the possibility of another sort of insight that is not limited by our contingent cultural commitments, and which is not a competitor with our best scientific understandings. As Kripal puts it, "Maybe an entirely different way of knowing is being called for here. Maybe these events cannot be explained because they are not caused through any ordinary physical channels. Maybe they are *expressions* of something. Maybe we should be reading them."[47]

These insights, if they really are distinct from both our scientific understandings (however well-grounded) and inherited mythological traditions, would not yield another "positive truth to measure and prove," nor will they bless us with "some new piece of folklore to believe." Rather, this openness to the insights of primordial experience (the Ur mythos) might be "a playful reminder that our present cognitive hardware and cultural software are simply not up to the task of understanding who we are and what (or who) the world is."[48]

---

[47] Kripal, *The Super Natural*, p. 192.
[48] Kripal, *The Super Natural*, p. 192.

In Kripal's view, these insightful experiences serve precisely to show us that our current worldviews (scientific and religious) are, even if complete in their own terms, not quite the whole story, and Aristotle seems to agree. We have seen Plato and Strieber come to the same conclusion in our previous chapter: we are cave dwellers. Indeed, Aristotle says elsewhere in the *Metaphysics* that the question of the meaning of being may never be fully closed: "Indeed, the question that was asked long ago, is now, and always will be asked, and is always giving rise to puzzles — namely, What is being?"[49]

Maybe the question of being remains open because there is another source, in addition to metaphysics and rational cosmology, to which we must listen (or "read" in Kripal's preferred hermeneutical idiom) in order to move beyond the philosophical puzzles, and that is why primordial mythical insights need to be allowed to express themselves in order to augment our rational sciences. That is, we need to be attuned to what might be trying to manifest itself to us from outside our cave.

I write this not only to note the felicitous congruence between Kripal's and Aristotle's methodologies in considering religion. That's all well and good, but there is a bigger point to be made. If we are to take C.D.C. Reeve's advice given in the epigraph to this chapter seriously, and I am inclined to do so, then being an Aristotelian is not merely to parrot Aristotle's out-moded cosmological theories.[50] Rather, to be Aristotelian is to take up his intellectual dispositions, which is to use the broadest possible range of human experiences to construct the broadest possible unified understanding of the world.

Doing so, as I believe Kripal shows us, will require an openness to taking certain phenomena seriously as vehicles of cosmological and theological insight that may not sit well with the sort of cultural conservatism that is often associated with Aristotelianism. That discomfort, however, might be the necessary expense of taking Aristotle seriously, instead of sticking to our own convenient caricatures of the Philosopher. All of this is to say that, in light of this and the previous chapter, both Ufology and classical philosophy have very good reasons for taking each other quite seriously.

---

[49] Aristotle, *Metaphysics*, 1028b 2-3.

[50] Though maybe Aristotle is not as far wrong as we might have once thought. See Rupert Sheldrake, "Is the Sun Conscious?" *The Journal of Consciousness Studies* 20, No. 2-4, 2020: 8-28.

Part 2:

Super Nature and Ontology Beyond the Cave: The Metaphysics of the UFO

3 UFO Realism and the Uber-Umwelt: A Model for a Revised Ultraterrestrial Hypothesis

"People mistakenly believe, he said, that a myth is an untruth. But myth is not that. A myth is that which is TRUER THAN TRUTH. It may not be that flying saucers represent visitors from outer space. But if large enough numbers believe it, then in some sense it will become truer than true, long enough for certain things to change irreversibly."

—Jacques Vallée, *The Invisible College*[51]

"Stepping between Umwelten, or at least trying to, is like setting foot on an alien planet."

—Ed Yong, *An Immense World*[52]

Jacques Vallée is a disciplined thinker. He is not given to extravagant speculation, and he seems throughout his vast corpus of published writings, lectures, and interviews to afford himself no more nor less in the way of conclusions than what is strictly implied by the premises of his

---

[51] Jacques Vallée, *The Invisible College: What a Group of Scientists Has Discovered About UFO Influence on the Human Race* (San Antonio, TX: Anomalist Books, 1975), p. 207.
[52] Ed Yong, *An Immense World* (New York: Random House, 2022), p. 15.

arguments—and he doesn't help himself to premises frivolously. I'm not aware of any place where he indulges in unrestrained speculation.

It might be surprising to hold up Vallée as a living paradigm of epistemic discipline, as he is one of the deans of the field of ufology (if not The Dean), an arena of research associated in the popular imagination with phantasmagoric speculation, cults, conspiracies, wishful thinking, manipulation by intelligence agencies, mental illness ("tin foil hats"), pop-culture grifting, Hollywood sensationalism, etc. Though this has begun to change (at least in the eyes of academia) through the efforts of the likes of Jeffery Kripal[53] and Diana Pasulka[54] (whose work we will discuss at length in the final part of this book), the world of UFO studies is not typically thought of as a hotbed of laudable epistemic and evidentiary scruples.

The fact, however, that a scientist with the highest academic credentials would suffer the consequences for his reputation by entering into such a fray (and publish accounts of his doing so) is part of my point. Vallée is one of the most "follow the evidence" people you could ever find. Moreover, he is not bashful about criticizing the state ufology, despite his high standing in that community:

> Much of it is driven by motives that have more to do with political and publicity convenience, or just plain, opportunistic greed than with genuine research. It corresponds to a desire to influence the belief systems of younger generations, rather than a serious effort to preserve, and build upon, the accuracy of facts. And its reasoning is wholly based on shortcuts. Dangling the promise of "UFO Disclosure" is as good a marketing strategy as any, since progress cannot be measured by any realistic standards, and there is no defined end point to the research.[55]

That being said, Vallée, however cautious of deception and grift, has persisted in his ufological studies for over half a century. He clearly believes there is something worth his time in this phenomenon. If the data take us into a weird world of abductions, government psy-ops, and even elves and fairies (these are all topics he has considered rigorously at various points in his long career), then Vallée is willing to go there, even when doing so may lead to his being scorned or vilified by his elite peers. Encountering the rigor, honesty, and

---

[53] Jeffery Kripal, *The Super Humanities: Historical Precedents, Moral Objections, and New Realities* (Chicago: University of Chicago Press, 2022).

[54] Diana Pasulka, *American Cosmic: UFOs, Technology, Religion* (New York, Oxford University Press, 2019).

[55] Jacques Vallée and Paola Harris, *Trinity: The Best Kept Secret* (Mansfield, MA: Starworks Publishing, 2022), p. 52.

circumspection of Vallée's work is part of what led me to start taking the Phenomenon seriously as an avenue for philosophical reflection.

Vallée has been steadfast for decades in claiming that the data show almost unquestionably that *something significant* is going on regarding UFOs. The sheer quantity of reported sightings and the non-negligible proportion of those that defy ordinary explanation together demand serious explanatory inquiry rather than a dismissal as mere aberrations or background noise in the data. As Vallée puts it in one of the canonical texts of ufology:

> There is one haunting thought underlying the UFO phenomenon: *something* mysterious seems to be manifested in our environment—the "things" have been seen by thousands of people in all countries. They have been tracked on military radar, and they have been photographed by astronauts, leading many to the belief that they originated in outer space. They have been filmed by rocket-borne cameras and touched by farmers. They have been adored by simple people, denied by scientists, prayed to by the devout, cursed by primitives and celebrated by poets. They have been called Flying Saucer, Unidentified Flying Objects, Uncorrelated Targets.[56]

For Vallée, the empirical question of whether there is a UFO phenomenon was already settled affirmatively when he wrote those remarks in 1975, and that case has only become stronger in recent decades.[57] Thus, let's take it *that* there is a UFO phenomenon as our point of departure, and turn to the question as to *what* that phenomenon might be.

Vallée's take on this question has been remarkably consistent throughout his decades of confronting the issue, even though he is ultimately non-committal as to the nature of the UFO phenomenon, which is an expression of his admirable epistemic discipline. He gives what I take to be the most concise statement of his subtle position in *Five Arguments Against the Extraterrestrial Origin of Unidentified Flying Objects*, a paper he first published in 1990 and later appended to his book *Revelation: Alien Contact and Human Deception*. (In the following, I will refer to the latter version).

Let's call anyone who believes that UFOs are actual entities that defy our ordinary categories of explanation *UFO realists*. The UFO realist is then claiming that the phenomenon demands an increase in our ontological commitment. That is, in addition to the the things we ordinarily enumerate on our list of real beings, e.g., bears, mountains, trees, human beings, electrons,

---

[56] Vallée, *The Invisible College*, p. 11.

[57] I believe the best account of the cumulative case to the effect that the UFO phenomenon cannot be dismissed is provided by Ross Coulthart, *In Plain Sight: An Investigation into UFOs and Impossible Science* (New York: Harper, 2012).

love, viruses, wrestling matches, etc., the UFO realist will also count UFOs as an additional category of beings.

Of course, this doesn't mean that all the items on our ontological list are the same kind of thing, but they are all real things, e.g., love and mountains are different kinds of things, but they are both realities. Thus, we should not fall quickly into the trap of thinking the UFO is at all like any of the other things in our inventory of the real as it previously stood. That cautionary note must be kept in mind for all of our subsequent discussion in this book.

A UFO *anti-realist* is then anyone who denies UFO realism, i.e., she does not believe that UFOs demand our positing another ontological category. For example, the most common version of UFO anti-realism is what Vallée calls the "natural phenomena hypothesis," according to which "all the reports can be explained as a combination of observing errors, classical atmospheric phenomena, and man-made objects, and possibly combined with little-known psychological illusions which are of no relevance to physics."[58]

On this view, since we already have such things as atmospheric phenomena (the infamous swamp gas!), projective illusions, secret government technology, etc., in our accounting of things, the UFO phenomenon does not demand that we add another ontological category. The UFO anti-realist does not deny that experiencers are seeing something, even something that appears quite anomalous, but she argues that these appearances are deceptive and can be accounted for without addition to our mundane list of things.

According to the UFO anti-realist, the UFO is merely an appearance of or construction from things already in our inventory of the universe. All that is needed, for the UFO anti-realist, is an account of how the phenomenal appearances of UFOs can be reduced to standard elements of our ontology.

Of course, this presumes that we have some pre-given, settled ontology, but surely that's not really the case. For example, a religious believer already committed to the existence of angels and demons might account for UFOs as cases of such entities. Would that claim be an expression of UFO realism or anti-realism? The religious person accounting for UFOs as angels or demons isn't adding anything to *her* ontology, but of course a lot of people don't recognize angels and demons as real beings.

To avoid such tough questions, let's say a UFO realist accounts for UFOs by adding an ontological category over and above those we would expect just about anybody would to accept. I don't think most believers in angels and demons expect just about everyone to share this view, so someone

---

[58] Jacques Vallée, *Revelations: Alien Contact and Human Deception* (San Antonio: Anomalist Books, 2015), pp,. 240-241.

claiming UFOs are angels or demons is then a UFO realist.[59]

Ockham long ago wisely advised that we ought not generate ontological categories frivolously, and Vallée would certainly be inclined to err on the side of anti-realism, *if* the evidence allowed him to do so. Nevertheless, despite his well-placed ontological stinginess, Vallée believes that the ship has simply sailed with respect to UFO anti-realism. Vallée has a great deal of sympathy for an explanation of the UFO in terms of psychological and archetypical projection, but that does not account for the empirical nitty-gritty of the phenomenon.[60] Even Carl Jung, the master of projective explanation, resisted resting comfortably in such a conclusion, because the phenomena leave such clear physical traces and therefore support some sort of realist interpretation.[61]

Moreover, Vallée does not deny that many of the reports are occasioned by encounters with secret government technology or even intentional psy-ops by intelligence services, but here too these explanations do not address the most salient cases.[62] Thus, UFO realism should be our grudging conclusion. It is implausible to suppose that we can reduce the UFO phenomenon to anything in our standard, everyday ontology. At least I am willing to operate under the working assumption of UFO realism. Any reasonable look into the evidence will show that UFO realism is plausible enough (even if not entirely probable) to warrant the efforts to construct an interpretive model, which is what I will begin in this and the following two chapters.

Does all this then commit the UFO realist to the claim that we have been visited by intelligent beings from another planet? Vallée believes that the inference to an affirmative answer is something of an unquestioned intuition among many (really, most) UFO realists, but it is a product of a hasty and unsound line of reasoning. This is not how Vallée puts it in his paper, but I believe it is a fair reconstruction of the implicit argument he is criticizing:

(1) Either UFO realism or UFO anti-realism.

(2) If UFO realism, then the Extraterrestrial Hypothesis (ETH) is very likely true.

---

[59] For such an account, see Charles Upton, *Alien Disclosure Deception: The Metaphysics of Social Engineering* (Sophia Perennis, 2021).

[60] See Vallée, *The Invisible College*, pp. 15-38.

[61] See Jung, *Flying Saucers: A Modern Myth of Things Seen in the Sky,* pp. 109-111.

[62] See Vallées, *Messengers of Deception: UFO Contacts and Cults* (Brisbane, Australia: Daily Grail Publishing, 2008) and *Revelations*.

(3) UFO anti-realism is untenable.

Therefore: (4) UFO realism is most likely true.

Therefore: (5) ETH is very likely true.

That's a fine argument, except that there are very good reasons to doubt premise (2). Vallée defines the ETH as the claim that "UFOs are physical devices controlled by intelligent beings from another planet who are visiting earth as part of a scientific survey, very much in the fashion we ourselves plan to follow in exploring remote planetary environments."[63] In other words, the ETH is the standard "It's little green men from Alpha Centauri" explanation.

Certainly, (2) is strictly false, i.e., there are other possible versions of UFO realism such that a commitment to UFO realism as such does not itself entail that one must accept the ETH. For example, Vallée himself seems to have some sympathy for the proposal that UFOs are interdimensional or wormhole travelers[64], and he is very suggestive of what he calls the control system hypothesis.[65] Moreover, in "Five Arguments Against the Extraterrestrial Origin Unidentified Flying Objects," Vallée makes a very strong case that the ETH is highly improbable given the data we have about UFOs as they appear to us. Thus, it is hard to say that (2) has anything going for it.

As the title of his article indicates, Vallée makes five arguments against ETH. I find all of these arguments fairly strong, but the most important for me is the case he makes based on the reported physiology of the beings (organisms?) supposedly operating these craft:[66]

> The vast majority of reported "aliens" have a humanoid shape that is characterized by two legs, two arms, and a head supporting the same organs of perception we have, in the same number and general appearance. Their speech uses the same frequency range as ours, and their eyes are adapted to the same general segment of the electromagnetic spectrum. This indicates a genetic formulation that

---

[63] Vallée, *Revelations*, p. 241.

[64] See Vallée, *Revelations*, p. 254-255.

[65] See *The Invisible College*, pp. 194-206. The control system hypothesis is the primary focus of chapter 5 of this book.

[66] This is a case Vallée continues to make this case even in his most recent work, see *Trinity*.

does not appear to differ from the human genome by more than a few percent.[67]

> It should be kept in mind that the human shape has evolved in response to an extremely narrow set of constraints. . . . How, then, can we expect that extraterrestrial visitors from a completely different planetary environment would not only resemble us, but breathe our air and walk normally on the earth?[68]

All of that is to say the notion of an entirely separate evolutionary process producing bipedal, forward looking, oxygen breathing, featherless, rational animals is so improbable as to strain credulity. *Maybe* there are as-yet unknown principles of evolution that pipeline things toward bipedal, featherless, and very smart animals. Or *it can't be ruled out* that the aliens might be so smart that they could genetically manipulate themselves to be adapted to our environment.

I'm in no position to dismiss such ancillary hypotheses for the ETH in principle, but I do worry that without some independent evidence for these claims we are coming close to rendering the ETH unfalsifiable. When one gets to positing extra principles of evolution and omniscient/omnipotent aliens for no other reason than to defend her hypothesis, her position is starting to lose traction in the real world. What could even count as counter-evidence, if one is willing to posit special powers or principles to account for it?

For example, if I want to explain how Smitty could have committed crimes in New York and Los Angeles within two hours (something in itself highly unlikely) by positing that he must have had a hypersonic aircraft, then it is far from clear what could convince me that I was wrong about his guilt. I'm willing to complicate my hypothesis to the highest degree to maintain my position. Avoiding this falsifiability problem increases the evidential demand. I can claim that my conviction in Smitty's guilt is reasonable, only if I can give some evidence that he actually does have a hypersonic aircraft.

Notice, however, that adding this further hypothesis hurts as much as it helps; it increases the evidential demand. This also applies to the ETH: unless it is to be relegated to a phantasmagoric just-so story, we are owed some reason to think evolutionary options are so limited and/or aliens really would be so smart and powerful. In other words, these ancillary hypotheses need independent evidence to keep the ETH from spinning into unfalsifiable triviality, and I fear that evidence is, as yet, still outstanding (though I could be

---

[67] Vallée, *Revelations*, p. 248.
[68] Vallée, *Revelations*, pp. 248-249.

corrected!). Thus, we do well to look elsewhere for a UFO realism model.[69]

Maybe we can find such a model a bit closer to home. Indeed, some ufologists entertain various versions of the *ultraterrestrial hypothesis* (UTH), according to which "sequestered terrestrial cultures . . . existing alongside us in distinct stealth" are responsible for the anomalous phenomenon we are encountering in UFOs.[70] Some of the proposals entertained within the UTH are that UFOs are technology wielded by a breakaway civilization of human beings or even some other species that evolved before us (that's why they're far ahead of us in terms of technology). Maybe these ultraterrestrials have always been in our neighborhood while perennially keeping an eye on us, or maybe they were alerted of or have become more concerned with our presence since we got our hands on nuclear weapons. In any event, the point of the UTH is that the "visitors" are not that distant from us on the evolutionary chain—they are earthlings! Thus, it is not surprising that we share much the same gross anatomy and biochemistry, and that they construct what we can recognize as artifacts and technology.

Notice, however, that the UTH, like any hypothesis, is going to come at the expense of further auxiliary hypotheses, which will likewise raise the evidential price for this conclusion. For example, the advocate of the UTH will owe us an explanation as to how the ultraterrestrials have managed to remain hidden from us for so long, why they are showing themself now (or being detected), etc. etc. We will be forced to account for their intentions and their nature, though they are, according to the hypothesis, hidden from us. Any attempt to answer these questions by positing special powers or intentions on the part of the ultraterrestrials will get us into similar problems to what hampered the ETH advocate's attempt to defend her position. It will render the claim either unfalsifiable (omniscient/omnipotent ultraterrestrials or special natural processes that cannot be disconfirmed) or call for independent evidence for the ancillary hypotheses that is not forthcoming. Thus, as it stands, I'm not convinced the UTH really buys us much over the ETH.

That being said, I want to aver a proposal in the vicinity to the UTH, though with far less evidential commitment. The following proposal, what I call the *Uber-Umwelt Terrestrial Hypothesis* (UUTH) is a version of UFO realism, i.e., it claims we are bumping into something real and *sui generis* with respect to

---

[69] We might wonder why so many bright people in the ufological world have been so quick to help themselves to the false dichotomy embedded in premise (2), especially when doing so requires such evidential special pleading. As is so often the case, there is an air of an implicit orthodoxy that is holding us captive in such cases, and this is an issue we will discuss at length in chapter 6.

[70] H.E. Putoff, "Ultraterrestrial Models," *The Journal of Cosmology* Vol. 29, No. 1: https://thejournalofcosmology.com/Puthoff.pdf (accessed, May 21, 2023)

our other ontological categories when we encounter the phenomenon—the UFO is something from outside our cave. Nevertheless, the UUTH is based on a well-known explanatory concept (the *Umwelt*) employed fruitfully in biology, phenomenology, cognitive science, and the philosophy of mind, so it comes already armed with a good bit of independent confirmation from its explanatory success in those fields.[71]

In short, the central explanatory concept of the UUTH is both non-trivial and the beneficiary of independent evidential backing. Thus, I think we can avoid the problems encountered by the ETH and standard versions of the UTH by taking the UUTH seriously. Notice, however, *this is not an attempt to demonstrate the UUTH.* That work can only be done by painstaking empirical investigation, and that's nothing that I can do from the comfort of the philosopher's proverbial armchair. I am only attempting to show that the UUTH is plausible and circumvents the shared problems of the ETH and standard versions of the UTH.

In the early twentieth-century, biologist J. von Uexkull introduced the notion of the *Umwelt* (literally, "around-world") into sensory biology, which is typically, though maybe infelicitously, translated as "environment." Cognitive scientist Andy Clark unpacks what Uexkull has in mind by *Umwelt* as "the set of environmental features to which a given type of animal is sensitized."[72] As mentioned earlier, this notion has been well-tested across a variety of disciplines, e.g., sensory biology, cognitive science, and phenomenological philosophy.

---

[71] What follows in both this and the next chapter is an attempt to advance our understanding of the UFO phenomenon (and maybe a lot more!) by employing the tools of phenomenological philosophy, in particular Heidegger's fundamental ontology. I would never have thought to have done so, especially in applying these ideas to Vallée's work, had it not been for Diana Pasulka's *American Cosmic*, where she frames much of her project in these terms. Any of us who are now taking the UFO seriously from the comfort of academic armchairs owe a great deal to Pasulka's pioneering field work and subsequent analyses. Moreover, though he is not strictly operating in the phenomenological milieu, something along the lines of this model is implicit in some of what John Keel is proposing in his classic of ufology, *Operation Trojan Horse (San Antonio, TX: Anomalist Books, 1970).*

[72] Andy Clark, *Being There: Putting Brain, Body, and World Together Again* (Cambridge, MA: Bradford Books, 1998), p. 24. The title of Clark's book, *Being There*, is a thinly veiled reference to the notion of *Dasein* (literally, "there-being") in Heidegger's *Being and Time*, where the notion of *Umwelt* plays a central role in this influential phenomenological structure. The connection with Heidegger will become important as our inquiry progresses over the remaining chapters of this book.

Uexkull's famous example is a kind of tick whose sensory system is solely attuned to butyric acid (emitted by the skin of mammals), surface pressure (good for detecting when one has landed), and heat (good for detecting when one is close to a blood source). These three sensory factors allow the tick to time its jump onto an approaching mammal, find a good place to bite, and get the blood it needs to survive. The important point is that the full richness of the sensory factors available in the physical world is narrowed to three affordances that *matter* to the tick. The tick's perceptual capacities are not ordered to "getting" the whole world, but only the world in the aspects that make a difference for it, and that means the tick's perceptions leave behind more than they take in.

As we discussed earlier, perception sorts for relevance. The *tick's* environment (*Umwelt*) of perceptual concern is then determined by the interplay between its needs and strategies for serving those needs. The whole *world-for-the-tick* is the collection of objects as defined in terms of butyric acid, surface pressure, and heat, and they constitute a nicely convenient cave for the tick. That is not to say that the world beyond butyric acid, surface pressure, and heat don't exist until something needs them. The tick's physiology and behaviors (even its very needs) are formed by a dialectical history of interaction with these present factors. The idea is that the broader world is not part of the tick's perceptual environment, because it isn't relevant to its needs (or at least it plays no role in its survival strategy—for good or ill).

None of that vast beyond is really a concern for the tick, so it's off the tick's radar. Certainly, the tick could be eaten by a non-butyric-acid emitting being, say, another insect, but that object would be an irruption into the comfortable *Umwelt* of the tick. The tick-eating insect would be from the *Uber-Umwelt* (super-environment) of entities utterly alien to the tick's *Umwelt*. The tick-eaters are "out there," but they don't matter much to the ticks in the sense that they don't show up in the tick's sensory environment in a way that they can proactively deal with. There are also all sorts of non-threatening factors in the *Uber-Umwelt* relative to the tick, e.g., the green of the blade of grass on which it sits. The only world available to the tick is the *butyric acid-surface pressure-heat world*, which is certainly a mere sliver of what there is. The poor tick is missing out on a lot! Here is how Clark puts it well:

> Von Uexkull's vision is thus of different animals inhabiting different effective environments. The effective environment is defined by the parameters that matter to an animal with a specific lifestyle. The overarching gross environment is, of course, the physical word in its full glory and intricacy.[73]

---

[73] Clark, *Being There*, p. 25.

The point of all this is that an organism's framing of the world in terms of its perceptual capacities (its *Umwelt*) is limited to those factors that are relevant to its survival strategies, which always results in something of a narrow caricature of the full richness of a perceived object. For example, when the tick senses a human being, its framing of her is entirely in terms of butyric acid, surface pressure, and heat. What a crude reduction! These factors are far from exhausting the being of a human, but that is how the tick frames us. The fullness of our being is in the *Uber-Umwelt* with respect to the tick. That is not to say that the tick gets us *wrong* (our butyric acid, surfaces, and heat are perfectly real), but only that it has a narrowly skewed picture bent toward its needs, and this skewed framing (though effective) is far from the whole story. We only appear as a shadowy image on the walls of the tick's cave.

Notice, however, that there are caricatures in both directions—our picture of the tick is no less skewed to our needs. There are indefinitely (infinitely?) many available factors in any situation to which an organism can be attuned, and the whirl of perceptual possibility has to be sorted in order for any animal to be able to take effective action, i.e., animals must determine an *Umwelt* for themselves (through their evolutionary history), and humans are no exception.

Moreover, like other animals, we are leaving much behind in the *Uber-Umwelt* in order to get a practically workable framing. Maybe our five senses (and subsequent conceptualizations) are richer than the tick's, but we no-less winnow down the world to what is relevant to our needs. We're pretty aloof to all that butyric acid we are huffing from our neighbors. Our perception of the tick is then likewise a shallow caricature of the fullness of its being. The tick only appears as a shadowy image on the walls of our cave! Once again, this is not to say that our perceptions (and subsequent conceptualizations) get the tick wrong, but only that they fall short of the full being of the tick, and this is true of all the objects of our perceptions: we are only scratching the surface of their being in our perceptual encounters, because our senses, though attuned to the world, are ultimately self-serving. In short, our *Umwelt* is a subset of the vast *Uber-Umwelt* that constitutes the world, and we can rule out neither that there is much more to those objects we do perceive nor that there are objects far beyond our convenient framings.

Maybe that conclusion is a bit troubling. What else, hiding in the *Uber-Umwelt*, might be in this room with me right now? Think of ticks and the tick-eating insects. Such bugs might be hidden in the *Uber-Umwelt* relative to the tick, even though the latter might be prey for the former. We aren't necessarily attuned to all the threats we could suffer. What might my desk really be up to in its far richer being in the *Uber-Umwelt* beyond my limited perceptual access to it? The tick has no idea as to what we are up to in the *Uber-Umwelt* when it caricatures us in its *Umwelt* by sensing our butyric acid and heat. Who knows what goes on in the *Uber-Umwelt*?!

At the very least, we should not be surprised now, if the world is quite surprising. The factors in the *Uber-Umwelt* are "out there," but they are inaccessible to us under normal conditions, and I expect there are a lot of marginal cases. For example, clearly humans and the Portuguese Man of War can show up on each other's radar, but these are fairly rare occurrences, and we are very foreign (alien!) to each other. We aren't part of the mainstream of each other's *Umwelten*, so our encounters are as though we bumped into something from another world (*Welt*).

There are occasional irruptions from beings whose *Umwelt* and ours just barely overlap, and that is likely distressing both parties. Think of the case of sharks. In their ordinary everyday *Umwelt*, they are pretty much top-dogs. Outside the odd hapless surfer, I suspect we're mostly hiding out in their *Uber-Umwelt*. That is, until we show up in steel cages with dart guns looking to tag a shark or take it back to the lab. None of those factors have any ordinary role in the shark's *Umwelt*—we're reaching out to them mostly from the *Uber-Umwelt*.

The same might be true for a naive surfer who has strayed into the shark's territory. Sharks' and human beings' evolutionary history probably didn't overlap all that much, so our perceptual capacities are not all that attuned to each other. When we do encounter each other, often something is irrupting into our worlds from a much broader reality, which doesn't make sense in the framing we have evolved to manage things. I suspect, in our own incommensurably different ways, we both have a "What the hell is that?" moment, and there are very likely other far more alienating inter-*Umwelt* encounters than shark-human interactions. Human-shark encounters are inter-cave "communications."

The point I'm working toward should be readily clear. We need not think of the entities behind the appearances of UFOs as a hidden, breakaway civilization of humans (or human-ish beings) or humanoid extraterrestrial explorers. No, maybe the entities behind the UFOs are earthly beings (terrestrials who might have a very distant evolutionary link with us and the rest of the organisms on this planet), but they are hidden and elusive because they largely exist in the *Uber-Umwelt* relative to us. We simply have not evolved sensory capacities to get a hold of such beings with any depth, just as great white sharks and ticks haven't been set up to get us right in any real detail. That there are beings or aspects of beings in the *Uber-Umwelt* is something already strongly supported by the successes of the notion of the *Umwelt* as it has been employed in various other fields of inquiry.[74]

In short, the UFO realist adopting the UUTH is employing a type of

---

[74] See Ed Yong's brilliant *An Immense World*, pp. 3-16

explanation that already has some good evidential support. Moreover, we would expect our encounter with these *Uber-Umwelt* beings to be uncanny. UFOs are indeed beings from beyond *our world*, not our planet but our *Umwelt*. In the UUTH, the "aliens" have always been here, just like the sharks, ticks, bugs, Portuguese Men of War, and human beings, but our ordinary concerns (which shape our perceptual capacities) aren't aimed at them.

Thus, our marginal encounters with the beings from the *Uber-Umwelt* don't make much sense to us. In fact, our unconscious sense-making systems likely distort more than they reveal about the beings encroaching on our cave. Maybe our lives and the lives of these "aliens" are just indifferent. (We've been going our separate ways for all these eons, with the occasional very uncomfortable collision.) Maybe they hunt us. (How attuned are codfish to human beings?) Maybe they have a better or deeper take on us and they are curious. (Catch and release?) Might they be running things? (Do ants in a kid's ant farm have any notion of their master?) Those questions are left for future empirical work, but they don't need to be answered to get the probability of the UUTH off the ground. In other words, we don't need to come up with an additional auxiliary hypothesis to explain the hiddenness, opacity, and uncanniness of beings erupting from the *Uber-Umwelt*. All of that is intrinsic to the basic concepts grounding the hypothesis. Thus, the UUTH promises considerable explanatory power, but at a much lower overall evidential cost than either the ETH or standard the UTH.

This proposal allows us to bring all order of supernatural and paranormal phenomena into the explanatory mix, and explanatory unification is a good sign for a model. What are ghosts, fairies, DMT elves, etc? They aren't mere constructions out of our already existing ontological categories. No, they really do come from "beyond." They are not, however, supernatural in the traditional sense, though I would say they are supernatural in the older sense I detected in Aristotle in the last chapter, i.e., ghosts, elves, demons, and the like are a part of *nature*, but it turns out that nature is *super*!

Nature is not limited to the *Umwelt* of our mundane, practically oriented perceptual capacities. Our cave is not the ultimate measure of what Being has to offer, and when we are lucky or unlucky enough to run into something from the *Uber-Umwelt*, things get very spooky. Obviously, this all sounds a lot like Kripal's notion of super nature, and that is no accident. I see the UUTH as a proposal that could be expanded into a fruitful way of framing Kripal's proposed research program. We might do well to investigate all well-evidenced "paranormal" phenomena (UFOs and otherwise) as irruptions of the *Uber-Umwelt* into our *Umwelt*. To that end, in the following chapter, I will further develop the *Uber-Umwelt* hypothesis using the resources of recent work in Object Oriented Ontology and the related notion of a hyperobject.

4 Unidentified Flying Hyperobject: Thinking Beyond the Goldilocks Ontology

"But then we have to ask, of course, what this class comprises. We are given, as examples, 'familiar objects'—chairs, tables, pictures, books, flowers, pens, cigarettes .... But does the ordinary man believe that what he perceives is (always) something like furniture, or like these other 'familiar objects'—moderate-sized specimens of dry goods?"

—J.L. Austin, *Sense and Sensibilia*[75]

"There are many senses in which a thing may be said to 'be', but they are related to one central point, one definite kind of thing, and are not homonymous .... and unity is nothing apart from being; and if, further, the essence of each this is one in no merely accidental way, and similarly is from its very nature something that is: all this being so, there must be exactly as many species of being as of unity."

—Aristotle, *Metaphysics*[76]

"What, for example, is the size of IBM, or the Red Army, or the French Ministry of Education, or the world market? To be sure, these are all actors of great size, since they mobilize hundreds of thousands or even millions of

---

[75] J. L. Austin, *Sense and Sensibilia* (New York: Oxford University Press, 1962), p. 8.
[76] Aristotle, *Metaphysics*, trans W.D. Ross, in *The Complete Works of Aristotle* Vol. 2 (Princeton, NJ: Princeton University Press, 1984), 103a33

agents . . . Yet there is an Ariadne's thread that would allow us to pass with continuity from the local to the global, from the human to the nonhuman. It is the thread of networks of practices and instruments, of documents and translations . . . . The only difference stems from the fact that they are made up of hybrids and have to mobilize a great number of objects for their description . . . . [T]he modern world appeared disenchanted, drained of its mysteries, dominated by sleek forces of pure immanence on which humans alone imposed some symbolic dimension and in which there existed, perhaps, the transcendence of the crossed-out God. Now if there is no immanence, if there are only networks, agents, actants, we cannot be disenchanted. Humans are not the ones who arbitrarily add the 'symbolic dimension' to pure material forces. These forces are as transcendent, active, agitated, spiritual, as we are."

—Bruno Latour, *We Have Never Been Modern*[77]

"A model does not assert that something is so, it simply illustrates a particular mode of observation."

—Carl Jung, *On the Nature of Psyche*[78]

In our common folk ontologies we tend to privilege what J.L. Austin famously (at least among analytic philosophers) called "moderate-sized specimens of dried goods." For example, if I were to ask my son Cormac to enumerate all the *things* in our backyard on a spring afternoon, he would probably produce a list including the black walnut tree, the garage, the various toys left out, his older brother cutting the lawn, the lawnmower, the flowers, the bees, and probably the odd garter snake or two scared out into the open by the lawnmower.

Notice, however, that Cormac's list would, strictly speaking, leave a lot out! For example, there are legions of very small things out there that he would likely fail to include, e.g., the bacteria in the soil, the oxygen atoms in the air, and the photons radiating from the sun. Moreover, Cormac would likewise leave out a great many abstract things that are, *in some sense*, in the yard, e.g., *the green* of the trees, *the mass* of the bees, and *the width* of the yard itself. Sure, qualitative and quantitative attributes aren't the *same sort of things* as

---

[77] Bruno Latour, *We Have Never Been Modern*, trans Catherine Porter (Cambridge, MA: 1993), pp. 118-119, 128.

[78] C.G. Jung, *On the Nature of Psyche*, trans R.F.C. Hull (Princeton, NJ: Princeton University Press, 1960), p. 94.

bees and trees, but they *are things*. Trees, bees, and yards cannot exist without attributes (*being in* certain qualitative and quantitative *ways*), so the latter have some sort of being along with the former.

Thus, if we are going to give a very strict accounting of what is out the backyard, we should probably count both the entities that have attributes and the attributes that are had by those entities. Leave aside for our purposes whether qualitative attributes like *green* are in the yard or in our consciousness (or both!), or even whether the yard is actually "out there." Those are certainly legitimate philosophical worries, but we can't deal with every philosophical conundrum all at once; as it has been said "Each day has evil sufficient unto itself." Let's assume a sort of naive realism about all that, for now at least.

I also doubt that Cormac would include bigger things, such as the utility company that owns the power lines or the neighborhood association organizing the weekend's block party (in preparation for which his older brother is cutting the lawn). Nevertheless, these *organizations* are in some sense present (at least through their effects); the *being of the utility company* and *the being of the block association* are necessary parts of the explanation of what is going on in the yard. Once again, utility companies and neighborhood associations aren't the same kind of things as power lines, lawnmowers, or older brothers, but they are things *in some sense*. Utility companies and neighborhood associations make a difference for the activities of power lines and older brothers, so we can't outright deny them *thing-hood*. If it were not for the action of the utility company, then the power lines wouldn't be out there, and it's the planning of the neighborhood association that occasions the lawn-cutting.

If something has an effect, then it must *be*, in one way or another, along with the things it is influencing. As my dissertation advisor used to remind me: "Everything is a thing. It's just a question of how we order them." Moreover, if something is having an effect in some locality, then it must be somehow present in that place. Thus, the utility company and the neighborhood association are in the backyard, but certainly not the same way as the walnut tree and the blades of grass.

We have, however informally, been engaging in what philosophers call *ontology*, a term I helped myself to without much explanation in the previous chapter. Part of ontology is to come up with a complete inventory of all the *things* that there are. *Prima facie*, that's an impossible task—there are trillions upon trillions of things, if not infinitely. There could be no such piecemeal inventory of what there is! Fair enough, but really in ontology, we are after an inventory of *categories* of things, and even at that we are most concerned with getting at the most *fundamental categories* of things. Thus, a philosopher is not out to count the number of cats in the backyard (though there are some famous cases of that), but whether "cat" is a *bona fide* category of thing, or merely an attribute or effect of something else. Beyond those sorts of questions about what is basic among our categories of things, ontologists tend to let the scientists and other specialists sort things out in terms of the specifics.

Thus, a philosopher doing ontology is not after the particulars, but the *kinds* of things that inhabit the universe. As you have already seen, philosophers take "thing" in the broadest possible sense. For example, I picked on Cormac's ontological inventory of the backyard for his failure to include subatomic particles, attributes, and organizations. Moreover, there are quite prominent philosophers who argue that we need to include the categories of *fictional objects* (e.g., Hobbits) and *merely possible objects* (e.g., the older brother I never had, but might've). Should we include minds? Historical events? Future events? Numbers? Angels? As you know, these become very sticky questions in a hurry, and controversies abound.

Thus, ontology is not a simple inventory, but something that requires a principle for inclusion or exclusion in our list of basic categories. That is, the point of ontology is to develop some sort of theory of what it is for something to be at all, so that we can give a non-arbitrary accounting of our basic categories of being.

Let's call this knee-jerk preference for moderate-sized dried goods the *Goldilocks Ontology*, as it privileges concrete things (as opposed to abstract entities) that are neither too small (particles like photons) nor too large (organizations like the utility company), and note that we all share this tendency at the level of common sense. If Cormac had included the oxygen and the utility company, we would likely have found that correct, though a bit odd. Moreover, the Goldilocks Ontology is philosophically well-credentialed, at least going back to the first systematic ontological categorization in the Western tradition, Aristotle's *Categories*:

> [A] Of things said without any combination, each signifies either substance or quality or qualification or a relative or where or when or being-in-a-position or have or doing or being-affected. To give a rough idea, examples of substances are man, horse; of quantity: four-foot, five-foot; of qualification: white, grammatical. . . . [79]

> [B] A substance—that which is called a substance most strictly, primarily, and most of all—is that which is neither said of a subject nor in a subject, e.g., the individual man or the individual horse.[80]

> [C] . . . animal is predicated of man and therefore also of the individual man; for were it predicated of none of the individual men it

[79] Aristotle, *Categories*, in *The Complete Works of Aristotle* Vol. 1 (Princeton, NJ: Princeton University Press, 1984), 1b25-30.
[80] Aristotle, *Categories*, 2a12-17.

would not be predicated of man at all. Again, color is in body and therefore also in an individual body; for were it not in some individual body it would not be in body at all. Thus all the other things are either said of the primary substances as subjects or in them as subjects. So if primary substances did not exist it would be impossible for any of the other things to exist.[81]

Those are rather torturous passages (standard Aristotelian fare!), but we can make sense of them pretty easily. In [A], Aristotle is asserting the "everything is a thing" principle we discussed above. He is saying that among *the things that are*, we must include not only substances like humans or horses, but also attributes, e.g., qualities, quantities, relations, etc. A full accounting will include individual *beings* and the *ways* in which they *are being* (attributes): *the grass* that is green, and *the green* that the grass is. The term "substance" is loaded with controversy and ambiguity in this context, but, for our purposes, we can take it to mean simply an individual, concrete thing such as *a* human being or *a* horse, as opposed to the color or quantity of humans or horses.

In [B] Aristotle asserts that substances are the privileged ontological class: the most fundamental things are individual concrete entities like a man and a horse, to their attributes (what he calls here "qualifications"). These points may seem rather tedious, i.e. individuals are more fundamental than their attributes, but this is really Aristotle picking a fight with his mentor, Plato, and that is a debate we don't need to wade into for now.

With [C], Aristotle is giving an argument to support his assertion in [B]. As I put it to my students, you can never step in a pile of *brownness* or *grammar*, but you will know it when you step on a brown horse or a grammatical man! Attributes are always the attributes *of something else, a human* or *a horse*. In other words, things like *four-foot* or *white* are always dependent on more basic concrete *things* that *are four-foot* (a four foot long snake) or *are white* (a white tiger). Thus, Aristotle concludes that attributes are secondary with respect to the primary beings, i.e., individual concrete substances—Austin's moderate-sized dried goods.

Notice, however, that Aristotle leaves some pretty obvious concrete individuals off his list of fundamental substances. No artifacts (whereby "artifact" we mean an artificial as opposed to a naturally occurring things) appear among Aristotle's list of substances in the *Categories*. He would recognize Cormac's older brother as a substance, but not the lawnmower he is pushing. Moreover, Aristotle does not mention the finer-grained constituents that compose humans and horses (for Aristotle, this would be earth, air, water, and fire, but for us it's whatever sub-atomic particles we're currently

---

[81] Aristotle, *Categories*, 2a36-2b6.

64

supposing to be the ground floor), which come in their own concrete instances. One might also note that Aristotle doesn't mention things like the utility company or the neighborhood association. He only seems to have in mind individual, living beings such as *a human* or *a horse*. Where then do elements, artifacts, and organizations fall on Aristotle's hierarchy of beings? What might justify Aristotle's exclusion of these things (if he does exclude them) from his inventory of basic categories of being?

> One of the places he addresses this question (or at least develops resources for addressing it) is in his *Physics*:

> [D] Of things that exist, some exist by nature, some from other causes. By nature the animals and their parts exist, and the plants and simple bodies (earth, fire, air, water)—for that these and the like exist by nature. All the things mentioned plainly differ from things which are not constituted by nature. For each of them has within itself a principle of motion and stationariness (in respect of place, or growth and decrease, or by way of alteration).[82]

> [E] On the the other hand a bed and a coat and anything else of that sort, *qua* receiving these designations—i.e., in so far as are products of art—have no innate impulse to change. But in so far as they happen to be composed of stone or of earth or of a mixture of the two, they *do* have such an impulse, and just to that extent — which seems to indicate that nature is a principle or cause of being moved and of being at rest in that to which it belongs primarily, in virtue of itself and not accidentally.[83]

Aristotle's point in [D] is that natural things (living things and elements) are ontologically privileged because they can *do their own thing*. A living being does not merely *passively* accept the fate of entropy, but *actively* pushes back against the forces of nature that tend toward equilibrium and chaos. Organisms take steps to keep themselves organized in the face of the decomposing pressures surrounding them (at least for a while). A plant, for example, moves itself through its natural process of development (an internal principle of "motion") and in doing so resists the tendency of matter (at higher levels of organization) to fall back into decomposition (an internal principle of "stationariness").

Likewise, in Aristotle's view, elements are not merely passive playthings of other beings, as they dictate their own definite set of processes

---

[82] Aristotle, *Physics*, in *The Complete Works of Aristotle*, Vol. 1, 192b9-15.

[83] Aristotle, *Physics*, 192b15-23.

and changes. For Aristotle, *something that does its own things is its own thing*, i.e., beings that act on their own are not merely dependencies of other things, but substances in their own right. In short, if something can move itself (independent development) and maintain itself, then it is a substance, a member of a basic category. Elements and organisms are just such self-movers and self-maintainers. The basic things *do their own thing*.

In [E], Aristotle points out that artifacts, say the chair I am sitting on as I type this essay, are not self-movers and self-maintainers. The chair does not actively dictate any distinctively chair-like changes or processes of its own. A chair is simply accidentally arranged wood, screws, fabric, etc. It is only going through wood, metal, and fibrous changes (really just slow decomposition), not distinctively chair changes. Chairs don't *do their own thing*, but are merely along for the ride as they piggy-back on their constituents.

Thus, Aristotle would say that artifacts like chairs are merely *accidental beings*, i.e., they are *attributes of* or *ways of being of* their constituents. The additional fact that something is a chair adds notion to the principles of self-motion and self-maintenance of the wood and metals that compose it. Thus, elements and organisms have ontological pride of place relative to artifacts.

Of course organisms are composed of elements, but Aristotle believes that living things are not merely along for the ride for three primary reasons: (i) Living things undergo changes wholly absent at the level of their elements, e.g., metabolism, sensation, cognition, etc.; (ii) living things can maintain their identity through the incremental replacement of their elemental parts, i.e., through the normal course of metabolism living things will change out all of their material constituents while maintaining their identity; and (iii) living things have a certain control over their elemental constituents, i.e., the organism as a whole has a downward effect on the behavior of its constituent elements.

In short, since there are distinctive effects of organisms over and above the effects of their elemental constituents, Aristotle concludes that organisms are their own things (substances), even though they do have a kind of dependence on their composing elements.[84] We can see then that the basic principle of Aristotle's ontology is that things that move/maintain themselves in ways novel with respect to their parts, have their own identity with respect to their parts (they can survive the loss/gain of their parts), and have some kind of control over their parts are substances.

---

[84] The ontological integrity of organisms, like just about everything in philosophy, is controversial. For a defense of this kind of non-reductive view of organisms informed by recent biology, see Evan Thompson, "Life and Mind: From Autopoesis to Neurophenomenology," *Phenomenology and Cognitive Science*, 2 (2004): 381-398.

Aristotle he does take certain organizations as things that "happen according to nature" (that's the subject of his *Politics*). He thinks of families, villages, and cities (the highest level of social organization that Aristotle thought that could be reasonably maintained!) as natural objects that happen no less on their own than the developments of organisms and elements. Moreover, social organizations can survive replacement of their parts, e.g., the city will change from one generation to another. So far, it seems like organizations are on their way to the hallowed title of substance.

Aristotle, however, does not believe that families, villages, and cities do their own thing, because, unlike organisms with respect to their composing parts, we run the organizations we compose. Aristotle sees families, villages, and cities as under the conscious rational control of their rulers. In short, even though organizations are things in *some rather strong sense*, e.g., Aristotle would say that your family or your neighborhood have a higher ontological standing than your toaster, they are not basic because they are not running the show for themselves independently of their parts.[85] The traditional view is that organizations are just relational beings piggy-backing on the substances that compose them, e.g., a city is just a relation (a shared attribute) held among its residents. The city does not run itself, let alone its constituent human beings, especially (for Aristotle) the members of its ruling class. Thus, something akin to the Goldilocks Ontology finds is original philosophical justification in Aristotle, who would basically agree with Cormac's ontological accounting of things in the backyard, so long as he properly degraded the standing of the lawnmower and other artifacts and gave proper place to the elements.

There is no dearth of available philosophical critiques of the Goldilocks Ontology. Indeed the entire modern materialist program can be seen as an attempt to undermine the notion that moderate-sized entities have any standing over and above their micro-sized constituents. More interesting, for our purposes, is not such critiques "from below" (worries that Aristotle gives too much credence to moderate-sized objects relative to their micro-sized constituents), but what I'll call critiques "from above" (worries that Aristotle does not give macro-sized objects enough credence relative to moderate-sized constituents). For example, Graham Harman (a present-day ontologist) is happy to defend moderate-sized objects from reduction to their composing elements (what he calls *undermining*), while he argues that we have been too quick to privilege middling beings over the "larger" objects they compose. Harman recognizes:

> entities at every scale of existence without dissolving them into some ultimate constitutive layer. A specific Pizza Hut restaurant is no more or less real than its employees, table, napkins, molecules, and atoms of

---

[85] See Aristotle's *Politics*, Bk. I, Ch. 1-2.

which it is composed, and also no more or less real than the economic or community impact of the restaurant, its headquarters city of Wichita, the Pizza Hut corporation as a whole, the United States, or the planet Earth. All these entities sometimes affect and are affected by others, but they are never exhaustively deployed in their mutual influence, since they are capable of doing other things or even nothing at all.[86]

Harman's point is that an equally strong case can be made for the ontological independence and integrity of objects like restaurants, cities, corporations, economies, etc. relative to their constituent entities as can be made in favor of organisms as standing over their elemental components. That is, in the same way Aristotle saves moderately-sized objects from their micro-sized components, Harman defends macro-sized objects from their moderate-sized components. As he puts it, "an object need not be physical, solid, simple, inanimate or durable; it need only be irreducible either downward to its components or upwards to its effects."[87] If a thing has effects novel with respect to its components (including control of those components) and an identity that survives their replacement, and it controls its parts, then that thing is real—*without qualification.*

That's the basic case Aristotle makes regarding organisms, and Harman would simply have us apply it consistently to the organizations, institutions, extended events, etc. that have moderate-sized beings (including *us!*) as their constituents: if these composite objects have causal powers (including "downward" control) and identities of their own, then they have *bona fide*, unqualified ontological standing as substances. Though he is a fan of Aristotle's defense of moderately-sized objects, Harman parts company with him when it comes to organizations like the neighborhood association and the utility company.

Using the examples of the Dutch East India Company and the American Civil War, Harman makes a very detailed case for the ontological standing of macro-sized objects.[88] Even without wading into those fascinating details, it's not hard to motivate this position intuitively. Take Harman's example of a particular Pizza Hut restaurant. Certainly, the restaurant as a system has novel effects relative to its composing parts, i.e, that equipment,

---

[86] Graham Harman, *Immaterialism: Objects and Social Theory* (New York: Polity, 2016), pp. 16-17.

[87] Graham Harman, *Object Oriented Ontology: A New Theory of Everything* (New York: Pelican, 2018), p. 114.

[88] See Harman, *Immaterialism*, pp. 35-95 and *Object Oriented Ontology*, pp. 114-134.

staff, building, etc., cannot bring about Pizza Hut effects without their incorporation into the restaurant. If all the employees go work for Walmart, the ovens are sold off, and the building is demolished, at some level all the parts survive, though there won't be any more pizza being produced.

Moreover, the restaurant has a sort of effective control over those constituents, e.g., the employees (including the management supposedly running the place) all behave differently in virtue of their incorporation into the system. Even the management is constrained in what they can do with the restaurant by the whole they partially compose; their decisions making is different in virtue of their employment in that particular Pizza Hut. There can even be a mood or spirit of a particular restaurant that affects the performance of the employees differently from other franchises. Finally, that particular restaurant can outlive the incremental replacement of all its composing elements. The entire staff, management, and equipment can be changed over while we still have the same Pizza Hut restaurant. Sadly, your local Pizza Hut may outlive all of its current staff.

In this way, we can make a case that a particular Pizza Hut has *a life of its own*, and a similar argument can just as well be made regarding objects on even larger scales, such as corporations, cities, nations, planets, etc. The exclusion of these much bigger, organizational beings from Aristotle's list of fundamental substances now looks rather arbitrary. It turns out that Pizza Hut is running things, at least in its corner of the world. If Harman's position has traction, and I think it does, then *things we originally do or set in motion*, e.g., a Pizza Hut franchise, can actually *go their own way* independently of us, and even while controlling us. A Pizza Hut is an artifact, but it also seems to take on its own "internal principle of motion and stationariness."

Moreover, we might now have nested hierarchies of *bona fide* substances, some of which are hybrids of natural beings and artifacts. For example, each employee is both a *bona fide* substance, while they are incorporated into the restaurant, which is itself a *bona fide* substance. That restaurant is also a constituent of the Pizza Hut corporation, which also has a life of its own. Thus, Cormac would have done better to include the utility company and the neighborhood association among the objects "in" the back yard. At least those things have their own ontological standing and the reach of their tentacles has an effect on the other things in the yard.

If we now put all objects with their own powers and integrity of identity on equal footing (the micro, the moderate, and the macro), we might wonder how big things can get. Timothy Morton makes the case that things can get VERY big. He uses the the term:

> . . . *hyperobjects* to refer to things that are massively distributed in time and space relative to humans. A hyperobject could be a black hole. A hyperobject could be the Lago Agrio oil field in Ecuador, or the

Florida Everglades. A hyperobject could be the biosphere, or the Solar System. A hyperobject could be the sum total of all the nuclear materials on Earth. . . . A hyperobject could be the very long lasting product of direct human manufacture such as Styrofoam or plastic bags, or the sum of all the whirring machines of capitalism. Hyperobjects, then, are "hyper" in relation to some other entity, whether they are directly manufactured by humans or not.[89]

Thus, a single object can be so massive as to dwarf us; not only spatially or temporally, but also *cognitively*. Things, even things we get started, can take on such vast or complex lives of their own as to operate on scales we can hardly, if at all, fathom. What is the sum total of plastic in the world really up to? If it forms a system, is that a system we really understand, let alone control? Might THE PLASTIC be running us now to some degree, in the way Pizza Hut Inc. is running its management and staff? A case can be made that the environment is a hyperobject. Can we have a grasp of such a complicated and vast being? Here's how Morton puts it:

> [Hyperobjects] are *nonlocal*; in other words, any 'local manifestation' of a hyperobject is not directly the hyperobject. They involve profoundly different temporalities than the human-scale ones we are used to . . . . Hyperobjects occupy a high-dimensional phase space that results in their being invisible to humans for stretches of time.[90]

Employing the terminology I introduced in the previous chapter, hyperobjects mostly exist in the *Uber-Umwelt* with respect to us. The *Umwelt* is the perceptual environment an organism selects out of the fabulously rich set of possible framings of things based on its perceptual capacities and strategies for coping. Our human *Umwelt* is tuned for dealing with moderate-sized dried goods (relative to us!). The Goldilocks Ontology is the convenient selection of beings that we recognize by official cave-dwelling policy. Beings far surpassing that scale in size, time, or complexity exist almost entirely or completely in the *Uber-Umwelt* relative to us, outside the cave.

Thus, hyperobjects, inasmuch as we can encounter them at all, are only available to us at their extreme "edges." What we can sense, perceive, or even conceptualize regarding a hyperobject is merely a small fraction of their full being. Hyperobjects only show themselves to us in our caricatures of them, because they exist on a scale (temporally, spatially, and even in terms of complexity) we simply have not developed faculties to deal with. Notice, too,

---

[89] Timothy Morton, *Hyperobjects: Philosophy and Ecology at the End of the World* (Minneapolis, MN: University of Minnesota Press, 2013), p. 1.
[90] Morton, *Hyperobjects*, pp 1-2.

that what shows up for us in our *Umwelt* as many distinct things, might actually be manifestations of one object operating in what Morton calls "a higher-dimensional phase" or what I call the *Uber-Umwelt*. Each individual Pizza Hut restaurant is really just the manifestation of the Pizza Hut corporation, which is something we can only encounter around its edges. It looks like we are encountering *many things* (and in some sense we are—the individual Pizza Hut restaurant is there!), but behind (or above or beyond) those manifestations there is a single object running that show for itself through those manifestations.

We encounter encounter *a* snow storm or *a* tornado, but we don't ever get in direct touch with *the* environment running these weather events far beyond our meager perceptual screens. We can go see a particular line at the unemployment office or watch the ticker representing the latest foibles on Wall Street, but we have no direct access to *the economy* of which these phenomena are expressions. No *single* video of carnage is *the* war in Ukraine. It might even be that things like economies, environments, and wars are so vast as to be beyond our grasp and control. The limited "snapshots" are all we have access to, while the full reality of the hyperobjects lurks out there in the *Uber-Umwelt* running its own life.

That possibility is particularly interesting, since economies and wars are in some sense human doings, and the environment seems to be something we can affect. Nevertheless, these effects of our own activities can take on the lives of hyperobjects such that in encountering them we are running into something of which we have wholly lost control, an Other. What is the war in Ukraine really up to out there in the *Uber-Umwelt*, now that we have let it out of the café? Is the financial crisis of 2008 really gone, or lurking outside the cave? I don't think we can say that the U.S. Civil War has exactly gone away.

Even though some hyperobjects have their origin in processes originally loosed by humans, there is a sense in which "the reality is that hyperobjects were already here, and slowly but surely we understand what they were already saying. They contacted us."[91] In other words, we might initiate things that evolve to such a scale that we will eventually encounter them, or be "contacted" by them, as beings on their own and operating in a realm that is actually beyond our ken.

The UFO phenomenon is famously uncanny. It is hard to make any sense of it in terms of just "nuts and bolts" technology, but it clearly is not only a psychical or paranormal phenomenon. Maybe the UFOs don't fit neatly into any of our categorizations because we have been thinking of them exclusively as discrete individuals, not unlike our aircraft or space ships, that should be characterized on one side of the natural vs. artificial dichotomy. That is, maybe our default preference for the Goldilocks Ontology gets in the

---

[91] Morton, *Hyperobjects*, p. 201.

way of entertaining the full scope of ontological possibilities we need in order to make sense of these phenomena.

What if UFOs aren't many, but one? Suppose we're not dealing with the UFOs, but THE UFO. Maybe THE UFO is a singular hyperobject that we can only encounter at its edges, just like we can only encounter the economy or the environment at its edges. That is not to deny the existence of the individual craft or what have you. Nobody denies the reality your local Pizza Hut or the tornado that wiped out your home, while maintaining that these things are the manifestations of much "larger" hyperobjective realities at work at scales that dwarf our comprehension.

We might make better progress in understanding THE UFO if we conceptualized the "individual craft" less like discrete individuals, and more like manifestations of a single hyperobject in the way we can think of snow storms and unemployment lines as the edges of much grander objects in the *Uber-Umwelt*. On this hypothesis, THE UFO is *one thing* doing *its own thing* on a scale far surpassing our human *Umwelt*. We get glimpses of it it along the edges (sightings of craft, encounters with seeming humanoids, etc.), but THE UFO exists mainly in our *Uber-Umwelt*, i.e., a singular thing operating so vastly as to boggle our minds, which are geared toward moderate-sized dried goods. THE UFO is neither moderately sized, nor is it a dry good (it is ill-behaved in light of our expectations for objects). The things outside our cave might be very large!

The most enticing part of this suggestion follows on Morton's notion that hyperobjects can be processes originally initiated by human beings, but which have taken on vast lives of their own. Could THE UFO, as a hyperobject, be something we initiated? Maybe in addition to economies, nations, wars, corporations, etc., our technological interventions have introduced hyperobjects into the world that are even more grand in scale and complexity than those better-known beings. Maybe we did something to get THE UFO off the ground in the first place, but now it's on the loose under its own steam, operating at levels far beyond our reckoning, and possibly producing manifestations that outstrip our ability to understand them.

It wouldn't have to be all our doing, much like the case of the environment and climate change: THE UFO as hybrid hyperobject. Certainly, the environment was "out there" before we showed up, but it seems that we have done things to interact with it that have moved it into a new and possibly novel phase wherein it behaves quite differently. Consider how some environmental thinkers have adopted the notion of the Anthropocene as a new geological age brought on by human interaction with the environment. We might see the Anthropocene as a hyperobject formed as a hybrid of the environment and human activity (mainly technology) that is up and running on its own. Morton seems to suggest as much, or at least the Anthropocene is an effect of such a hyperobject operating in its hidden vastness.[92]

Likewise, maybe there was something out there in our *Uber-Umwelt* minding its own business for eons, but at some point, we introduced a novel process that entered into a systematic relation with this previously aloof denizen of the *super-around-world*. The result is a symbiosis that has taken on a new life of its own, or at least our doings coaxed that hyperobject in the *Uber-Umwelt* in a new direction that shows up for us now in novel and uncanny dimensions. This might explain why THE UFO seems to have appeared rather rarely (though how is a matter of debate) until 1945 when it more frequently made itself known. We definitely introduced something unprecedented around that time, and that introduction may have been incorporated into a new being that has a powerful and unfathomable (to us!) life of its own (a hybrid hyperobject).

The idea is not that our technologies, in particular our nuclear ambitions, signaled to extraterrestrial beings that it was time to come look in on us more regularly, but that *we* initiated an entity that has taken on a life of its own (maybe by forming a hybrid with something already "out there" in the *Uber-Umwelt*) such that it now contacts us as an uncanny Other. Just because we don't know what's going on outside our cave does not entail that our activities cannot have profound effects on what is going on, or even exists, out there beyond our pale. In short, we might do well to consider whether we unwittingly contributed to the inception of THE UFO, though now we are forced to share our environment with this new-fangled hyperobject. Moreover, as Morton highlights, it is possible that even hyperobjects we played a role in creating have something to tell us. That is a theme we'll discuss at length in the final chapter.

Of course, I have no evidence to support the suggestion that THE UFO is a hyperobject, and I only offer it as a corollary to the Uber-Umwelt Hypothesis I introduced in the last chapter, which is itself merely a suggestion for reconceptualizing the question in what may be a fruitful manner. When our questioning keeps ending up in deadends, we need to examine our fundamental assumptions, especially the dichotomies that seem to be giving us the most trouble. This is why many of us think, the mind-body problem, a perennial philosophical impasse, demands that we rethink the very distinction between the physical and the non-physical.

Furthermore, the suspicion that our base assumptions might be wrong is part of what is motivating Jeff Kripal's proposal that we question the presumed dichotomy between the natural and the supernatural as we approach the study of the so-called "paranormal" in the humanities. Likewise, the roadblocks we keep meeting in our attempts to understand THE UFO

---

[92] See Morton, *Hyperobjects*, pp. 4-5.

may lead us to rethink not only our preference for the moderate-sized over the macro-sized, but even the distinction between the natural and the artificial.

5 MAGONIA AS HYPEROBJECT:
THE ORGANIC CONTROL HYPOTHESIS AND THE
RE-ENCHANTMENT OF THE WORLD

"But it may be that with this anchoring of ontology in a single ascetic dualism, thousands of gods are released into the woods, unnoticed."

—Graham Harman, *Tool Being*[93]

"For god, wanting to make the world as similar as possible to the most beautiful and most complete intelligible things, composed it as a single visible living being, which contains within itself all living beings of the same natural order."

—Plato, *Timaeus*[94]

"Beings, however, do not wish to be badly governed: 'To have many rulers is not good: let there be one ruler.'"

---

[93] Graham Harman, *Tool Being: Heidegger and the Metaphysics of Objects* (Chicago: Open Court, 2002), p. 99.
[94] Plato, *Timaeus* in *Timaeus and Critias*, trans. T.K. Johansen (New York: Penguin, 1965), 30d.

—Aristotle, *Metaphysics*[95]

". . . one is obliged to understand all motion, all 'appearances,' all 'laws,' only as symptoms of an inner event and to employ man as an analogy to this end."

—Nietzsche, *The Will to Power*[96]

"Could it be that our reaction to the reports, individually and collectively, is as much a part of the UFO phenomenon as the objects themselves?"

—Jacques Vallée, *The Invisible College*[97]

We've traveled a long way, and I want to pull together a lot of the strands that are running through the previous section of this book, so let's take a moment to summarize the territory we have recently covered. In chapter 3, I point out how Jacques Vallée argues strongly against the extraterrestrial hypothesis (ETH) as an explanation of the UFO phenomenon. The going alternative is the Ultraterrestrial Hypothesis (UTH), according to which the ontological grounds of the UFO phenomenon are not provided by alien species visiting Earth from another planet, but another species or race of highly advanced intelligent beings that have long existed right here on earth. The UTH has some advantages over the ETH, but, so I argue, it suffers many of the same difficulties, i.e., it forces us either to defend evidentially expensive ancillary hypotheses or relegate the UTH to unfalsifiable triviality by positing special powers on the part of the ultraterrestrials.

In that same chapter, I proposed my own explanatory framework, the *Uber-Umwelt Ultraterrestrial Hypothesis* (UUTH), as a friendly alternative to the UTH, though with the benefit of a greatly reduced evidential expense. The *Umwelt* is the "environment" of relevance an organism creates for itself based on its limited perceptual capacities and survival strategies. The idea is that our (along with all organisms') perceptual powers are not attuned to getting *everything* right, but only what is relevant to our particular needs and strategies. Thus, all perception leaves behind far more than it draws in, i.e.,

---

[95] Aristotle, *Metaphysics*, trans. C.D.C. Reeve (Indianapolis, IN: Hackett Publishing, 2016), 1076a4.

[96] Friedrich Nietzsche, *Will to Power*, trans. W. Kaufmann and R. Hollingdale (New York: Vintage, 1967), §619.

[97] Jacques Valee, *The Invisible College: What a Group of Scientists Has Discovered About UFO Influence on the Human Race* (San Antonio: Anomalist Books, 1975).

there is a vast *Uber-Umwelt* "out there" beyond our possible ken (outside the cave). This is a concept already well-credentialed in cognitive science, perceptual biology, and phenomenology, so the UUTH possesses sufficient evidentiary credentials (independent of its introduction into ufoology) to avoid the dilemma between triviality and evidential paucity. My proposal is to think of the ontological ground of the UFO phenomenon as something existing on the very edge of our *Umwelt*; a being mostly in our *Uber-Umwelt* with which we only have very occasional, and utterly uncanny, interactions.

In chapter 4, I furthered UUTH by adding the suggestion that the we consider the UFO phenomenon as a *single* hyperobject. A hyperobject is a being so vast in terms of space, temporality, and/or complexity as to be beyond the grasp of a "smaller" entity. In other words, hyperobjects exist mostly in the *Uber-Umwelt*, because their sheer magnitude (in the broadest sense) far outstrips our powers of comprehension. We only have access to hyperobjects along their "edges," i.e., limited manifestations of the whole that offer us the distorted appearance of being distinct phenomena. Of course, the parts of a hyperobject, at one level of analysis, can really be distinct things, though, at a higher level, they are manifestations of a greater unified whole (a substance) that is running things, e.g., tornadoes and snow storms as manifestations of the climate.

One of the important points to consider regarding hyperobjects is that they can be hybrid substances composed by a relation between something in our *Uber-Umwelt* and our own doings, e.g., the Anthropocene. Human activities might call into life hyperobjects that dwarf our own standing. On this view, anything with its own causal powers, identity conditions, and an influence on or control over its parts is a *bona fide* object, even if it was originally an artifact or caused "artificially," e.g., Pizza Hut, Inc. may have a life of its own that outruns our attempts to grasp or control it. Thus, *we might be unknowing manifestations of some hyperobject operating in a "higher phase,"* as Tim Morton puts it. That is, we could be constituents of hyperobjects that originate in our own doings, though now they exert their own organic control on us and defy our abilities to understand them at their in depth, e.g., the Great Depression or all the plastic in the world might be such hyperobjects.

The suggestion that THE UFO may actually be a hyperobject to which we have unwittingly contributed does much to explain, for example, the sharp uptick in manifestations of THE UFO following the Second World War: our poking around in the skies (and eventually outer-space) and utterly novel technological interventions in nature (most significantly the atom bomb) led to more frequent or qualitatively different interactions with something (someone?) in the *Uber-Umwelt*, and that interaction has taken on a hyperobjective life of its own.

Both the ETH and standard versions of the UTH posit explanatory entities that are more or less comfortably placed in our default Goldilocks Ontology of proverbial mid-sized dried goods: technologically advanced visitors from other planets or elusive earthlings wielding the same implements are concrete particulars of the sort we are used to dealing with. That is, the ETH and the UTH treat the ontological ground of the UFO phenomenon as though it were the kind of thing we are used to managing within our *Umwelt*, even if its powers and qualities greatly surpass those of the humdrum beings that ordinarily concern us.

These standard versions of UFO realism operate within the categories of our Umwelt, in much the same way that discovering an utterly new species of animal wouldn't knock us out of the cave. Even if such an organism were something bizarre like a surviving species of dinosaur, that encounter wouldn't shake our comfortable Goldilocks Ontology to the core. It makes sense that we would tend toward such explanations, since our *Umwelt* is the anchor point of all of our sense-making activities. Nevertheless, we should not trust ourselves too readily in this regard.

The fact that there is an *Umwelt* of things that make sense to us (through our particular strategies for perceptual and cognitive selectivity) entails there is always an even greater *Uber-Umwelt* that far surpasses our ordinary perceiving and thinking. Thus, *whenever we encounter something truly uncanny along with a tendency to package it among the mid-sized dried goods of our comfortable consensus ontology, we should be wary that we are likely simplifying or caricaturing things almost to the point of distortion.* That's just how we get around in the world!

Moreover, this tendency to keep our ontology in already domesticated territory is a cognitive liability of ours that could be easily exploited by those who might want to mislead or deceive. We need to be suspicious of our tendencies in this regard. Notice, however, by taking The UFO as a hyperobject, we are admitting as much, i.e., we are accounting for the fact that this being is something that operates almost entirely in our *Uber-Umwelt*, and therefore we are guarding ourselves (though not infallibly) against our natural tendency to "cut things down to our size." This ontological humility is one of the prime virtues of the UUTH that I am trying to motivate.

With all those considerations in place (albeit tenuously!), I want to return to Vallée's own preferred explanatory proposal for the UFO phenomenon, the *Control Hypothesis* (CH). In what follows, I will attempt to synthesize Vallée's CH with the UUTH, using the notion of the hyperobject as the key point in the maneuver. In short, by taking Vallée's Magonia as a hyperobject (maybe even a hyperobject of which humans have always been oblivious constituents), we are able to provide a broad explanation along the lines that Vallée has in mind with his original CH. Moreover, I will argue that this suggestion allows for an even smoother synthesis for those looking to connect the UFO phenomenon with the broader phenomena of what Jeff

Kripal calls Super Nature and some of the notions drawn from classical Greek philosophy that I introduced in the first part of this book.

Vallée introduces the control system hypothesis by first reiterating that "when we speak of UFO sightings as instances of space visitations, we are looking at the phenomenon on the wrong level."[98] Rather than thinking we are "dealing with successive waves of visitations from space," Vallée suggests we "are dealing with a control system."[99] Notice already that Vallée is drawing our attention away from mid-sized dried goods and toward objects constituted as larger systematic wholes. He draws this proposal out in a bit more detail as follows:

> I propose the hypothesis that there is a control system for human consciousness. I have not determined whether it is natural or spontaneous; whether it is explainable in terms of genetics, of social psychology, or ordinary phenomena—or if it is artificial in nature, and under the power of some superhuman will. It may be entirely determined by laws that we have not yet discovered.[100]

The proposal is motivated by Vallée's observation that the UFO phenomenon seems to be fraught with contradictory or incoherent elements: every intimation of "higher wisdom will soon be brought to naught by their insane incoherence or their calculated fallacy, even if they are couched in the higher language of tensor calculus."[101] In other words, the information experiencers gleam from the UFO phenomenon oscillates between the profoundly insightful and the infantile; the empirically undeniable and the utterly delusional; the rigorously scientific and phantasmagoric; the hopeful promise of a utopian future and the darkest portents of Armageddon.

The point, for Vallée, is not to reconcile all these *prima facie* contradictory claims. He doesn't think the meaning is to be found in the explicit information conveyed in these communications. There is a sort of "meta-logic" operating behind the contradictions, but it does not smooth out these tensions. The actual content of the messaging is superficial or at least ancillary to the real meaning of the UFO phenomenon. For Vallée, *the absurdity is the message*, because the point of reference for these locutions does not reside in our comfortable *Umwelt*. The purpose of these communications is not to convey information linguistically, but to get us to look for meaning in a different direction, outside the cave, and the way to do that is to leave us

---

[98] Vallée, *The Invisible College*, p. 195.

[99] Vallée, *The Invisible College*, p. 195.

[100] Vallée, *The Invisible College*, p. 196.

[101] Vallée, *The Invisible College*, p. 200.

perplexed as long as we persist in thinking of the issue in cave-dwelling terms.

Vallée sees in this dialectic of reason and the absurd the same pattern employed by classical, behaviorist conditioning, which operates by a *"schedule of reinforcement"* combining *"periodicity with unpredictability."*[102] In other words, Vallée argues, based on his vast analysis of the actual cases, that the UFO phenomenon gives every appearance of *training* us, just as B.F. Skinner famously trained pigeons and monkeys using operant conditioning, for the sake of some end that lies beyond our ordinary ken, in the *Uber-Umwelt.*

Skinner's methodological behaviorism has fallen out of favor among psychologists and philosophers of mind since Vallée first published *The Invisible College,* but I don't think he has committed his hypothesis to a shared fate with that particular psychological theory. In fact, after distancing himself from the typical stances of physicists or psychologists, Vallée identifies his approach as a *descriptive phenomenology* according to which "we will review what is experienced by the witnesses; we will observe what they do as a result of these experiences; and we will attempt to correlate them within a total framework."[103]

Phenomenology as a philosophical discipline comes in many varieties, but one of its most important variants takes our lived-world, what Edmund Husserl originally called the *Lebenswelt* or *lifeworld,* as the primary point of focus for investigation. This approach should be fairly familiar to us now, in light of our forgoing discussion. The idea is that understanding something is not *only* to catalogue its properties as quantified in some abstract system (physics), but to ask after its *meaning* as a clue to its *being*—or at least such a clue is the closest *we* can get to its being.

These phenomenologists argue that everything we say and do only has intelligibility against the background of an unspoken, and maybe unspeakable, *lifeworld* of practical meaning and significance. There are elements of our *Umwelt,* necessary to our understanding of anything, which we cannot literally put down on paper. As Hubert Dreyfus puts it, "most of what we experience must remain in the background so that something can be perceived in the foreground."[104] We have an understanding of or contact with reality which is implicit in our practices and activities, and those implicit meanings are the key to our having a grip on the world. We can only get a sense of this lifeworld by a careful analysis of what we do and reading between the lines of what we say. Our lifeworld is what gives us primary contact with reality, not our explicit abstract theories. Thus, understanding something is not fully achieved by considering it in terms of science (physical properties) or

---

[102] Vallée, *The Invisible College,* p. 199. Author's emphasis.

[103] Vallée, *Invisible College,* p. 3.

[104] Hubert Dreyfus, *What Computers Still Can't Do* (Cambridge, MA: MIT Press, 1992), p. 240.

introspective psychology (consciousness), but also in terms of what our unstated practices and activities reveal.[105]

We have as much to learn about the world by excavating the implicit meanings of what we say about it and how we treat it, as we do in our explicit theorizing. We might say that the phenomenologist is looking for signs of what things may be in the *Uber-Umwelt* by drawing our attention to what lies implicit and unstated in our *Umwelt*. Maurice Merleau-Ponty, the influential French phenomenologist, makes these point as follows:

> Phenomenology is the study of essences, and it holds that all problems amount to defining essences, such as the essence of perception or the essence of consciousness. And yet phenomenology is also a philosophy that places essences back within existence and thinks that the only way to understand man and the world is by beginning from their "facticity." Although it is a transcendental philosophy that suspends the affirmations of the natural attitude in order to understand them, it is also a philosophy for which the world is always "already there" prior to reflection—like an alien presence — and whose entire effort is to rediscover this naive contact with the world in order to finally raise it to "exact science," but it is also an account of "lived" space, "lived" time, and the "lived" world.[106]

Thus, when Vallée proposes a careful analysis of the effects of UFO experiences on our behavior and guiding attitudes, he is not indulging a crass behavioristic reductionism. Rather, Vallée is acting as a phenomenologist, who takes the phenomenon's effect on the lifeworld of the experiencer (and subsequently its effect on *our* lifeworld in general) as a clue (however ambiguous and opaque) to its being. In short, by asking what *the meaning of the UFO phenomenon is to us*, we take a first step toward understanding *what it is*, because our primary contact to its essence (like all essences) is actually the *unstated* meanings in our practices and implicit attitudes that are formed these

---

[105] Of course, I'm moving irresponsibly quickly here. To see this point made in the full detail it deserves, have a crack at Husserl's *The Crisis of European Sciences*, trans David Carr (Evanston Illinois: Northwestern University Press, 1970) and the first division of Heidegger's *Being and Time*, trans John Macquarrie and Edward Robinson (New York: Harper Collins, 1962). For the less philosophically ambitious, see Hubert Dreyfus and Charles Taylor, *Retrieving Realism* (Cambridge, MA: Harvard University Press, 2015).
[106] Maurice Merleau-Ponty, *The Phenomenology of Perception*, trans Donald A. Landes (New York, Routledge, 2012), p, xx.

encounters.[107]

Thus, Vallée argues that we miss the point by focusing too much on UFOs as particular entities, for "they are the means through which man's concepts are being rearranged. All we can do is trace their effects on humans."[108] UFOs, in the proverbial nuts and bolts sense, are just one of an array of phenomena, e.g., fairies, elves, apparitions, and all the other earlier denizens of Vallée's Magonia, serving the higher-level reality that is running this control system. In short, for Vallée, the important ontological question is not about the UFO *per se* (as the concrete, "nuts and bolts" entity that confronts us), any more than the question is about the fairies *per se*. These entities (real though they may be) are merely the means to some higher-level end, and Vallée is attuned to the biases of the Goldilocks Ontology.

The worry is *what* is behind the control system of which these beings are manifestations, and we can only start to understand that by considering how these encounters are altering our lifeworld. For Vallée, UFOs "are constructed as *physical craft* (a fact which has long appeared to me undeniable) and as *psychic devices*, whose exact properties remain to be defined."[109] If the UFOs are psychic devices, then the real question is not about the devices or machines themselves, but what end they serve as such equipment. Here is how Vallée makes the same point elsewhere:

> Indeed it may be that its manifestations are not spacecraft in the ordinary "nuts 'n bolts" sense. The UFOs are physical manifestations that cannot be understood apart from their psychic and symbolic reality. What we see here is not an alien invasion. It is a control system that acts on humans and uses humans. However, we still need to discover the source of this manifestation.[110]

UFOs are the means to some end, and their operation in a control system is the only clue we have as to what operates them (and to what end). Vallée is not doubting the concrete reality of the manifesting entities, but only their priority in explaining the phenomenon. The fact that these beings manifest systematically in ways suggesting a mechanism of psychological control

---

[107] I should note too that even though Vallée evokes the phenomenological method in *The Invisible College*, it is Diana Pasulka's explicit casting of Vallée's work in Heideggarian terms in *American Cosmic* that did the most to bring this field inquiry into the space of academics in the humanities. Pasulka's work will have center stage in the final part of this book.

[108] Vallée, *The Invisible College*, p. 200.

[109] Vallée, *The Invisible College*, p 202. Author's emphasis.

[110] Vallée, *Messengers of Deception, Messengers of Deception: UFO Contacts and Cults* (Brisbane, Australia: Daily Grail Publishing, 2008), pp. 236-237.

implies that there is a higher-order being grounding that system, and that is the object of our questioning of the UFO. *The question concerning the UFO is the interrogation of the ontological ground of the manifestations of the control system, and our only clue to answering that question comes by observing the effects of the UFO on us.*

Part of what so strongly suggests the notion of control is a movement toward equilibrium that Vallée finds in the oscillations of the the phenomenon:

> The thermostat is a mechanism that stabilizes the relationship between our body temperature requirements and the changing weather outside. Similarly, UFOs may serve to stabilize the relationship between man's consciousness needs and the evolving complexities of the world which he must understand.[111]

> We have seen that the control system operates like a thermostat. It progresses by oscillations, drawing from the antagonism of fire and ice, warm and cold, evil and good, all myths for the feeble minds of men, equally bound by higher laws. For hot and cold are only relative to a mean, two appearances of a single fact, the motion of molecules. Few people have grasped both the physics and the beauty of this.[112]

The control system is maintaining a sort of homeostasis, just as an organism maintains its identity through a balancing act between opposites. Interestingly, the control system operating through the UFO phenomenon (and broader Magonia) maintains its identity by way of a sort of metabolism (or at least that is what I am proposing) by dictating a homeostasis of human consciousness: "I suggest that it is a human belief that is being controlled and conditioned."[113] In other words, the control system does this homeostatic work by conditioning human consciousness through the introduction of myths (appearances and rumors of fairies, elves, apparitions, UFOs) into the collective human psyche:

> Human life is ruled by imagination and myth; these obey strict laws and they, too, are governed by control systems, although admittedly not of the hardware type. If UFOs are having an action at that level it will be almost impossible to detect it by conventional means.[114]

---

[111] Vallée, *The Invisible College*, p. 2.

[112] Vallée, *The Invisible College*, p. 200.

[113] Vallée, *The Invisible College*, p. 201. Author's emphasis.

[114] Vallée, *The Invisible College*, p. 199.

What I do mean is that mythology rules at a level of our social reality over which normal political and intellectual action has no real power. At that level, time frames are long, of the order of a century, and evolution is slow and sure. Mass media, which are designed to give split-second images of transients (the noisier the better), miss the signal entirely. A society with an attention span of ten minutes (the interval between TV commercials) can have no concept of events that have begun when my grandfather was not yet born and will end after my grandson dies. But there are such long-term changes and they may be deliberate. They dominate the destiny of civilizations. Myths define the set of things scholars, politicians, and scientists can think about. They are operated upon by symbols, and the language these symbols form constitutes a complete system. This system is meta-logical, but not metaphysical. It violates no law because it is the substance of which laws are made.[115]

The idea here is that human endeavors are mostly regulated by our shared mythological background, something we can certainly see as one of the most important insights of Jung's work. Thus, the most effective way to regulate human behavior on the broadest possible scale would be through cycles of mythologization and demythologization, and this is what Vallée sees in the control system behavior of the UFO and broader Magonia. We are regulated, over very long stretches of time, by the mythological/de-mythological triggering of archetypes in our collective unconscious.

As I have been hinting, I believe we do well to adopt an organic model for our speculations regarding the ontology of the control system. In that model, mythology is a sort of suite of hormones that are introduced to regulate and guide the cells (human beings) in some organic system: various hormones are released under varying conditions to keep the system on track. In the way an organism overall is exerting control over the cells through the secretion of regulatory hormones, the control system maintains homeostasis by the "release" of mythological/de-mythological ideas. Be careful not to fall into what Harman calls the *overmining* fallacy of presuming that an object, let alone a hyperobject, is no more than its effects on us. An organism is "nothing more" than the organizational whole of its composing parts, but it has a life of its own over and above its specific effects on those parts. Likewise, Magonia has a life of its own, far outstripping our contact with it.

Notice, homeostasis is maintained not for the sake of the regulated entities, but in the service of the higher order entity they compose, e.g., the homeostasis of the organs is done in the service of the stable identity of the organ system, and organ systems are maintained for the sake of the organism.

---

[115] Vallée, *The Invisible College*, pp. 201-202.

All of this is to say that the CH implies that something operating through the control system maintains its identity (regulatory homeostasis) and exerts influence (control) over its elements, i.e., the control system appears to be the activity of a *bona fide*, substantial object. That is, we have good grounds to conclude that there is something, a *single unity,* operating through the control system, in the same way that Harman argues that the Civil War and Dutch East India Company were *their own things.*

There is something over and above the UFOs (and other "spooky" things that show themselves to us), which is to say that Magonia is an object. Notice that, even though I find it almost indispensable, talk of an object *behind* the control system is distorting. My proposal is not that there is some separate entity that runs the control system in the way that I drive my car. Rather, the idea is that *the control system is its own thing, doing its own thing.* There is no separate entity running an organism; the organic system is the being running the things that compose it.

Moveover, as Vallée points out in the long passage I quote above, Magonia operates on a scale that surpasses our impatient human comprehension, showing up in uncanny ways, which is to say that the control system is a hyperobject. I think we can see hints at such a view in remarks like this:

> . . . such sightings have been made in earlier times; similar effects have been described; even the UFO "occupants" appear identical to the denizens of medieval Magonia. This suggests a reality of mind, beyond whatever technology is activating UFO energy. I continue to regard this phenomenon as a manifestation of a reality that is larger and more complex than a simple visit by interplanetary travelers: the reality of Magonia.[116]

I might caution the otherwise epistemically fastidious Vallée regarding a too-quick jump toward positing "a reality of mind" behind the operation of the control system. An organism can mindlessly maintain its homeostasis. Moreover, the supposition that we are guided into that homeostatic dynamic by a manipulation of our cognitive dispositions does not alone entail that the hyperobject moving that process is itself operating by higher-order cognitive dispositions understood by an analogy with our own subjectivity. Things can have lives of their own without being conscious, and the temptation to think otherwise is part of our humanistic tendency, i.e., we assume that *being* is primarily *to be like us.*

Much of what we might learn from the UFO puts this dangerous (or

---

[116] Vallée, *Messengers of Deception*, p. 236.

at least myopic) humanist to question.[117] We might rightly say that "Pizza Hut Inc. has taken on a mind of its own," but this is not meant indicate that the corporation is literally a conscious subject (a center of feelings, thoughts, etc. understood in terms of such *human experiences*), but only that it is doing its *own thing*, i.e., it's out of our control and operating by its own principles. I would prefer to temper Vallée's claim to "Magonia is a hyperobject that has a life and trajectory of its own." *Magonia is doing its own thing, but it does that by manipulating us cognitively.*

Maybe Magonia is cognitive, but that is something for which we would need an additional line of argumentation, and the risk of anthropocentrism in these matters is grave. On this view, we (and much in our world) are constituents of Magonia, which maintains itself by regulating our cognitive function (and the behaviors that follow thereupon), but beyond that we don't get insights into the inner life of this hyperobjective entity.

Vallée himself entertains two theses regarding the ontology of the control system:

> This theory admits of two interesting variants: (i) an alien intelligence, possibly earth-based, could be training us toward a new type of behavior. It could be representing the Visitor Phenomenon of Whitley Strieber or some form of "super nature," possibly along the lines of a Gaia hypothesis. (ii) Alternatively, in a Jungian interpretation of the same theme, the human collective unconscious could be projecting ahead of itself the imagery which is necessary for our own

---

[117] Graham Harman offers a very helpful differentiation between his object oriented ontology (OOO), according to which objects (including Morton's hyperobjects) have a sort of life of their own, and panpsychism, according to which fundamental, non-living objects are literally conscious subjectivities, in *The Quadruple Object* (New York: Zero Books, 2011). Notice that panpsychism often operates according to an undermining fallacy and an anthropocentric/humanist bias, both of which are contrary to the main thrust of Harman's argument. Part of the point of OOO is to quit seeing *human subjectivity* as the model for everything, i.e., getting over our humanistic obsessions that have caused us so much trouble. Objects (and more of them than the Goldilocks Ontology would care to recognize) get on just fine in the *Uber-Umwelt* without us. It may be that the revelation of the vacuity of our humanistic narcissism is the central insight we can take away from the phenomenon. Please note that I am not claiming that Vallée is a panpsychist, but only that OOO critique is helpful in our discussion. Moreover, I see Vallée as sharing much of the anti-humanist spirit of Harman's OOO.

long-term survival beyond the unprecedented crises of the twentieth century.[118]

Taking Magonia as an organic hyperobject allows us to accommodate and synthesize both of Vallée's variants of the CH. On the one hand, if Magonia is a single hyperobject maintaining itself through the cognitive regulation of humans, we are in similar territory as the Gaia hypothesis or super nature, though I think we might do well to revisit Plato's notion of a world soul in the Timaeus, according to which the universe is a living organism composed of a hierarchy of lower-level living beings.

On the other hand, as we have discussed above, Magonia operates by the manipulation of the human collective unconscious (our broadest lifeworld). On this proposal, the world soul (Magonia) maintains itself via projecting for us mythological images and ideas. Now, Magonia is not strictly acting for "our own long-term" interests, but its *own*: Magonia is maintaining its homeostasis through mythological (cognitive) control exercised over us.

Notice, however, that under my hypothesis, we have a constitutive relation to Magonia, i.e., we are part of what composes it as a hyperobject with a life of its own. Thus, the line between our interests and those of Magonia is not entirely clear. Do the interests of the organs run contrary to those of the organ system? In any event, we can see that the proposal of Magonia as an organic hyperobject allows us to see the UFO phenomenon in a sense as the human collective unconscious projecting out in front of us, because on this model the collective unconscious is maintained by a hyperobject we partly compose.

There are many possibilities for how we might interpret our relation to Magonia the Hyperobject. As I have suggested before, on this model, it is possible that Magonia is something we have unwittingly brought into being by our interactions with the environment, much like we may have brought the Anthropocene or climate change as hyperobjects into being by our interactions with the environment. That would make sense of the steep uptick of UFO reports that has happened in the last three-quarters of a century.

We might, however, entertain that we have always been constituents of Magonia, but our more recent forays into the skies, atomic warfare, and host of other technological game-changers have caused the *uber*-organism to release something of an immune response; Magonia is adjusting itself, trying to restore homeostasis, after some of its constituents have overstepped their role in the organic whole. Magonia does this by honing our lifeworld in a direction necessary for its equilibrium. This hypothesis would explain both why there have always been occasional adjustments by Magonia (the cycles of

---

[118] Vallée, *Revelations: Alien Contact and Human Deception* (San Antonio: Anomalist Books, 2015), p. 254.

mythologization/demythologization) and why the homeostatic efforts seem to have increased in the last several decades. That is all rank speculation, and I can do little more to motivate any of those hypotheses. Attempts to get to what is in the *Uber-Umwelt* are always suspect. What I do find significant, however, is that this approach to the UFO phenomenon begins to move us toward a sort of re-enchantment of nature.

By enchantment, I do not mean the disposition to believe that there is a fairy in every hedgerow. As we discussed in chapter 2, Aristotle and Plato are pretty dismissive of that sort of talk, but they certainly have an enchanted view of nature. In their view, the natural world is an interlocking system of hierarchies, wherein each cosmic level is "moved" cognitively by the rational desirability of the next higher level. That is, Plato and Aristotle (though they differ in the details, and there are important differences between their views and what I am pushing in this essay) saw the cosmos as a system of embedded cognitive control systems (divinities), terminating in a single unifying being, i.,e., Plato's "The Good" and Aristotle's "the god."

For the Platonic-Aristotelian school, the cosmos is enchanted in the sense that all levels of being are "desirous" of the next level above, and they are therefore directed by that level. To understand nature, for these Greeks, requires us to take into account this quasi-conscious aspect of everything which is the moving principle of the universe as a whole. The cosmos is not indifferent, but contemplative and desirous. Each level of intelligibility doesn't necessarily have the interests of its constituents "in mind," but its own as it moves toward the next higher level. Nevertheless, the doings of each divinity serve the balance of the cosmic whole.

Of course, all of that is hard to swallow for those of us who have been reared in the mechanistic obsessions of the Enlightenment, but the UFO understood through the lens of the CH (at least as I have developed it here) goes some way toward suggesting that Plato and Aristotle may not have been as far wrong as their early modern critics thought. If we are indeed constituents of a hyperobject guiding us by cognitive suggestion, then we have some support for a revised version of Platonic-Aristotelian cosmology.[119]

---

[119] Though maybe there isn't a lot of revision required, as Plato goes out of his way in the *Timaeus* to claim that the cosmology presented there is a "likely myth." That is, Plato is not committed to the details of his cosmological story *per se*, but only the general model of a universe that is run based on a cognitive/desirous relations among lower-to-higher-levels of being. Plato was much more careful in his attempts to speculate about the *Uber-Umwelt* than he is typically given credit for. We might say, adopting an important distinction from the phenomenological idiom, that Plato's project is *ontological* (bearing on the broadest structures of experience as clues to the structure of being) and not *ontical* (taking a stance on one particular interpretation of those structures).

There is a sort of optimism in the Platonic-Aristotelian picture. That is, though they are polytheists in a sense (each level of intelligibility in the living cosmos is a divinity), Plato and Aristotle believe that there is an ultimate penthouse suite, i.e., a single unifying divinity ("The Good" or "the god") that guides all the lower "floors" of the cosmic building by its sheer nobility and beauty. The Good/The God is the source of all the downward cognitive signals that regulate the entire interlocking system of hierarchies of cognitive/desirous beings composing the living cosmos. The Good/the god, for Plato and Aristotle, is the mind (or even brain) of the organism that is the universe, and this cosmic mind unites all of the lower deities into a coherent and ultimately perfected system of intelligibility.

The universe operates for the sake of what is The Best. There is nothing in Vallée's CH that would require such a happy ending. It is difficult, however, when we think about it, to take seriously the supposition that there could be a building without a top-floor. But, of course, that could just be another case of our bumping into the limits of our own sense-making capacities. Be that as it may, Vallée and the Greeks seem to share a cosmological view that involves an enchanted universe, while they recognize that the show isn't being put on simply for our sake.

Maybe the UFO phenomenon is the reminder that will disabuse us of the humanistic pretensions that have long plagued us. This goading toward species-wide humility does not, however, necessarily entail a nihilistic form of anti-humanism: whatever Mangonia's intentions, it takes us as worth managing (talking to!). We can only come to surety on these points, if we can at all, by a continued vigilance in our observations of the effects of the phenomenon on our lifeworld.

In any event, you might understand what I'm doing here as an appropriation of the Plato-Aristotelian project to a OOO metaphysics for the purposes of a general theory of Magonia. That sort of appropriation is not entirely novel, even if it has been done for the sake of very different philosophical interests in the past. See Harman's "Aristotle with a Twist," *Speculative Medievalisms: Discography*, 2013: pp. 227-254.

Part 3:

The UFO and the End of the World: Thinking After *American Cosmic*

6 The UFO, Religion, and Our Epistemic Vulnerability: Diana Pasulka's Unheard Message for Ufology

"'Then also imagine that there are people along the wall, carrying all kinds of artifacts that project above it—statues of people and other animals, made out of stone, wood, and every material. And, as you'd expect, some of the carriers are talking, and some are silent.'

'It's a strange image you're describing, and strange prisoners. '

'They're like us.'"

—Socrates conversing with Glaucon, Plato, *Republic*[120]

"We knowers are unknown to ourselves, and for a good reason: how can we ever hope to find what we have never looked for? The sad truth is that we remain necessarily strangers to ourselves, we don't understand our own substance, we must mistake ourselves; the axiom, 'Each man is farthest from himself,' will hold for us to all eternity. Of ourselves we are not 'knowers.'"

—Nietzsche, *The Genealogy of Morals*[121]

---

[120] Plato, *Republic*, trans C.D.C. Reeve (Indianapolis, IN: Hackett Publishing, 2004), 514ab-515a.

[121] Friedrich Nietzsche, *The Genealogy of Morals*, trans Francis Golffling (New York: Anchor Books, 1956), p, 149.

"And if it is a mystery, we too have a right to preach a mystery, and to teach them that it is not the free judgment of their hearts, not love that matters, but a mystery which they must follow blindly, even against their conscience. So we have done. We have corrected Thy work and have found it upon miracle, mystery, and authority. And men rejoiced that they were again led like sheep and that the terrible gift that had brought them such suffering was, at last, lifted from their hearts."

—The Grand Inquisitor's Indictment of Christ, Dostoevsky, *The Brothers Karamozov*[122]

"Is she saying that all of religion is just some kind of *put-on*?"

That was a question one of my students asked while we were discussing Diana Pasulka's *American Cosmic* as part of a course I was teaching on the UFO and the philosophy of religion. My reply to this student was that her question betrayed both *a profound understanding* and *a profound misunderstanding* of Pasulka's book. On the one hand, my student is correct to think that Pasulka (though I doubt she would put it quite so crudely) sees religion as *some kind of put-on*, while on the other hand Pasulka is far from thinking that religion is *just* a put-on. This is no criticism of the bright young woman who asked this question. Again, she's getting something very right, and very deep, about *American Cosmic*.[123]

Moreover, my student understands something about Pasulka's work that has, as far as I can see, gone nearly unnoticed by the great lot of ufologists. Maybe "unnoticed" is the wrong word, as the problem UFology

---

[122] Fyodor Dostoevsky, *The Grand Inquisitor with Related Chapters from The Brothers Karamazov*, trans Constance Garnett (Indianapolis, IN: Hackett Publishing, 1993), p. 30.

[123] I do not intend this chapter as a book review of *American Cosmic*, and I am more or less presuming familiarity with that text on the part of the reader. In short, I am not going to spare you the benefit of actually reading Pasulka's book! I should also note that one of the central themes Pasulka keeps front and center (the triangular relation obtaining among the UFO phenomenon, religion, and technology) throughout here discussion (beginning with the subtitle of the book!), will go almost unconsidered in this chapter, though it will be a central theme of the next, along with the Heideggerian concepts she deploys in this regard.

has in comprehending Pasulka's work is not a matter of mere inattention, but a cognitive blindspot intrinsic to the ufologist's own deepest, meaning-constituting commitments. That is, the ufologist misses one of Pasulka's central lines of argument, because she is critiquing the very lens through which the ufologist sees the world *as a ufologist*.

In the same way you can't see your own eyeballs directly, the ufologist cannot comprehend the object of Pasulka's critique without stepping outside of his or her means of sense-making. Ufology is held captive by a certain picture that structures the very discourse of Ufology, and that implicit picture is what Pasulka has put under her powerful critical microscope. As Ludwig Wittgenstein puts it: "A picture held us captive. And we could not get outside it, for it lay in our language and language seemed to repeat it to us inexorably."[124]

I have a sense that Pasulka's intentions, like Wittgenstein's, are ultimately therapeutic, i.e., the picture that holds the ufologist captive is a constraint blocking her from seeing things (including the UFO!) as they are. The ufologist has constructed a cave for herself, and it's hard to see the way out. Thus, Pasulka provides an occasion to "let the fly out of the bottle," or at least she offers a timely caution to those of us on our way into the trap. Her cautionary critique, however, seems to have fallen on deaf ears among those who most need to hear it.[125] This implicit picture certainly helps the ufologist see something (and Pasulka emphasizes this frequently), but, like any lens, it enhances our vision only by simultaneously narrowing it.

Turn on your favorite UFO podcast that has hosted Pasulka. You will hear a great deal of excitement over her adventures in the New Mexico desert with "Tyler" and "James," and plenty of the speculative questions about the materials they recovered there.[126] Ufology has listened carefully to Pasulka's accounts of the connections between the early U.S. space program and occult

---

[124] Ludwig Wittgenstein, *Philosophical Investigations*, trans G.E.M. Anscombe, P.M.S. Hacker, and J. Schulte (Oxford: Blackwell, 2009), §115.

[125] This puts Pasulka in good company, as Wittgenstein was likewise quite skeptical that many of his readers would be receptive to his therapeutic efforts. See the prefatory remarks to his Philosophical Investigations.

[126] I realize this paragraph is not a paradigmatic case of conscientious scholarship, and there definitely are significant exceptions to the rule of thumb I'm using here. For example, Kelly Chase's work is outstanding in this regard (and many others!) Nevertheless, I believe this is an overall fair assessment of how *American Cosmic* has been perceived by the mainstream of ufology. Moreover, if you follow the world of UFO podcasting and media more generally, you might find that the glaring absence of any extensive engagement with Pasulka's work by some of the most popular voices in that space is quite revealing.

religions (Jack Parsons penchant for the occult *a la* Aleister Crowley). Seemingly miraculous cognitive downloads of groundbreaking scientific/technological discoveries reportedly originating from beings claiming to be extraterrestrials, and other data points indicating an undeniable physical or quasi-physical reality of the Phenomenon are standard topics of conversations surrounding *American Cosmic*.

Yes, Diana Pasulka is a *UFO realist*—she thinks there are good grounds for believing that the phenomenon we denominate as "the UFO" is no mere illusion—and she has major league academic credentials. Couple those facts with the data she brings to light in *American Cosmic*, and you can see why ufology has excitedly welcomed an aspect of her work. In short, the publication of *American Cosmic* by Oxford University Press, and all of the revelations contained therein, are indeed a significant confirmation of the legitimacy of ufology in academia. Indeed, as an academic, I probably would not be writing essays and teaching courses about the UFO phenomenon, had it not been for the legitimizing influence of Pasulka's work!

Let's call this aspect of *American Cosmic*, which mainstream ufology gets right to some significant degree, the *ontological thesis*. Pasulka's work does indeed confirm the ufologist's hunch that the phenomenon represents a significant addition to or revision of the ontology entailed by our standard, post-Enlightenment categorization of beings. Pasulka clearly agrees with mainline ufology that there is more under heaven and on earth than our consensus reality typically recognizes, though she is too subtle to make a simple-mindedly blunt affirmation in this regard: "Is it real or is it imaginary? What follows suggests that it is both."[127] Furthermore, the mainline ufologist's insistence on the nuts-and-bolts/extraterrestrial understanding of the UFO also pays a sort of obeisance to the very same post-Enlightenment ontology she is struggling to overcome. This is a revealing tension, maybe even a contradiction, at the center of ufology.

Pasulka's ontological thesis, however, is not really anything new in ufology. That's not to say that there isn't any new information in this regard in *American Cosmic* (there certainly is!), but the new information is confirmatory of many already existing tropes in the long-standing UFO lore. This fuels the temptation to take *American Cosmic* as a groundbreaking piece of UFO journalism, giving us fresh confirmations of the founding claims of ufology. The myopic obsession with Pasulka's ontological thesis by popular (even prominent) ufology reduces her work in exactly that manner, but there is something much more profound (and troubling) going on in *American Cosmic*. Notice too that *ufology seems to be most enticed by those aspects of Pasulka's work that most confirm the legitimacy of ufology*, at the expense of the deeper

---

[127] Diana Pasulka, *American Cosmic: UFOs, Religion, Technology* (New York: Oxford University Press, 2019), p, 16.

messages the book clearly conveys.

On the one hand, where Pasulka in effect says "Hey, there are world-class scientists deeply interested in the UFO, the space program has a long-time relation to the phenomenon, there are some 'crash materials' that have not been disconfirmed. . .," UFology hears the message loud and clear, and that probably has much to do with the fact that this message affirms ufology's *raison d'etre*. On the other hand, where she has less laudatory things to say about ufology, possibly distressingly subversive suggestions, the message does not seem to be received at all. Let's call this often unheard message of *American Cosmic* Pasulka's *genealogical thesis*.

If you take "genealogical" as a signal of Nietzsche's influence, you are correct. Nietzsche's head pops up not entirely infrequently in *American Cosmic*. The book opens with the epigraph, "Almost two thousand years and no new god" (Nietzsche, *The Anti-Christ*, §19)[128], and the introduction begins with "When you gaze long into the abyss, the abyss gazes also into you" (Nietzsche, *Beyond Good and Evil*, §146).[129] Pasulka sets the stage for her chapter on "James" (Gary Nolan), the consummate scientist, with "Do you believe then that science would have arisen and grown if the sorcerers, alchemists, astrologers and witches had not been their forerunners?" (Nietzsche, *Gay Science*, §300).[130] Moreover, Pasulka recounts in some detail a synchronicity experience she had at pivotal moment in her intellectual development involving a passage from Nietzsche's *Gay Science* (§277), and she returns to this same set of remarks by Nietzsche when the topic of synchronicity arises again.[131] By invoking genealogy, I don't mean merely that Pasulka adopts a few particular insights from Nietzsche (which she does to good effect), but that there is something *methodologically Nietzschean* in her *modus operandi*. Consider the following remarks from Nietzsche:

> I learned in good time to divorce the theological prejudice from the moral and the no longer to seek the origin of evil *behind* the world. A certain amount of historical and philological training, together with a native fastidiousness in matters of psychology, before long transformed this problem into another, to wit, "Under what conditions did man construct the value judgments of *good* and *evil*?" And what is their intrinsic worth? Have they thus far benefited or retarded mankind? Do they betoken misery, curtailment, degeneracy or, on the contrary, power, fullness of being, energy, courage in the

---

[128] Pasulka, *American Cosmic*, p. vi.

[129] Pasulka, *American Cosmic*, p. 1.

[130] Pasulka, *American Cosmic*, p. 51.

[131] Pasulka, *American Cosmic*, pp. 108-111 and pp. 177-178.

face of life, and confidence in the future? A variety of answers suggested themselves.[132]

Nietzsche is explaining his method for investigating the *origins* of distinctively Christian morality (though he thinks his results can be applied broadly to other religious-moral views), and he believes that articulating these origins will reveal something previously unnoticed (or maybe even actively suppressed) about the nature of Christianity. Nietzsche is a thoroughly historical thinker, who believes that the key to understanding something requires that we come to terms with *how it came to be*. This historical (or even historicist) approach to understanding cultural institutions is one of the cornerstones of modern academic thought. Our questions of "What is it?" require us further to ask "How did it come to be in the first place?" We have come to see the *process of becoming* as intrinsic to the *being* of a thing, and Nietzsche is one of the early methodological masters of this modern mode of thought.[133]

Notice that Nietzsche assumes that accounting for the coming to be of the notions of good and evil, the basic categories of Christian morality, can only be done in terms of something that predates the coming to be of these categories. If something truly and originally comes to be as X, then it must have (in some sense) come to be from something prior that is non-X. For Nietzsche, the genealogical process is both historical and psychological, i.e., he believes that by articulating the conditions under which a certain mode of

---

[132] Nietzsche, *The Genealogy of Morals*, p. 151.

[133] The origin of this historicism is, of course, complicated. Certainly, Darwin did much to move us toward seeing the *process of becoming* as intrinsic to *being*. For example, following Darwin we now classify species in terms of their lines of descent from common origins, as opposed to intrinsic-static properties. Hegel too has influenced a great deal of Western thought in this regard, and of course Marx should be mentioned too. Freud (think of *Civilization and Its Discontents* and *Future of an Illusion*) and Jung (who is generally revered in UFology) do a great deal to help us see that the backstory of our beliefs plays a much bigger role than we might expect. (By the way, Jung's *Flying Saucers: A Modern Myth of Things Seen in the Skies* is itself a significant genealogical investigation.) In any event, we see a contrast in modern historicism to Aristotle's eternal universe with its static species. For Aristotle, questions of origins only applied to individuals, and not species, and individuals are not proper objects of knowledge. We might then take the Christian doctrine of creation *ex nihilo* as the first move toward historicism, since it makes the question of how things got here significant. In any event, historicist/genealogical thinking is ingrained in modern thought, and a case can be made that Nietzsche's work did the most to make this method explicit.

belief came to be in a culture, we also have a diagnosis of the conditions that lead to it in the individual believer.

Nietzsche gives us a psychic version of Haeckel's "Ontogeny recapitulates phylogeny." Our collective human histories operate in the background of our individual psyches. We can see here in Nietzsche, whatever their disagreements with him (and each other!), an anticipation of the development of the notion of the unconscious (individual and collective) by Freud and Jung. Thus, for Nietzsche, the coming to be of Christian morality, must originate in something that is non-moral and non-Christian. More generally, Nietzsche's genealogical method explains something like a cultural institution (e.g., Christianity) outside of the categories that are foundational to that institution (the picture by which that institution holds us captive).

Thus, for Nietzsche, the explanation of something like Christianity as a phenomenon cannot be given in the explanatory categories offered by the Christian (speaking *as a Christian*). He's trying to explain why those categories came to be in the first place, i.e., why anyone came to hold them at all. Thus, Nietzsche doesn't explain Christianity in terms of divine inspiration, the movement of the Holy Spirit, the showing up on earth by the Second Person of the Trinity, the historical reality of Jesus of Nazareth's miracles, etc.

So how does this actually work for Nietzsche? Consider two more sets of remarks from *The Genealogy of Morals*:

> Now it is obvious to me, first of all, that their theory looks for the genesis of the concept *good* in the wrong place: the judgment good does not originate with those to whom the good has been done. Rather it was the "good" themselves, that is to say the noble, mighty, highly placed, and high-minded who decreed themselves and their actions to be good, i.e., belonging to the highest rank, in contradistinction to all that was base, low-minded and plebeian.[134]

> The slave revolt in morals begins by rancor turning creative and giving birth to values—the rancor of beings who, deprived of the direct outlet of action, compensate by an imaginary vengeance. All truly noble morality grows out of triumphant self-affirmation. Slave ethics, on the other hand, begins by saying no to an "outside," an "other," a non-self, and that *no* is its creative act.[135]

In his genealogical explanation of Christian morality, Nietzsche first posits a pre-Christian/pre-moral state of things, i.e., a time when "good" meant the exact opposite of what the Christian moralist means by that term. "In the

---

[134] Nietzsche, *The Genealogy of Morals*, p. 160.

[135] Nietzsche, *The Genealogy of Morals*, p. 170.

beginning," as it were, "good" named the aristocratic and the powerful, whereas, "bad" referred to the lowly, the weak, the shamed. Then, as we see in the second passage above, those "bad" people can no longer stand their lowly position, and they revolt by inventing a new sense of "good," one that makes meekness, humility, equality, etc., virtues rather than vices. Christianity is then the metaphysical/theological fable that justifies this vengeful reversal of value. In short, Nietzsche locates the origin of the Christian ethic of love and self-sacrifice in its opposite: hatred, resentment, and will-to-revenge.

Nietzsche's explanatory genealogies, whether they are deployed to account for Platonism, Christianity, or modern science, are famously speculative, if not outright fictitious. It seems that all Nietzsche gives us are plausible (or maybe just not impossible) just-so stories about how things could have gone so as to give us something like Christianity. There is a worry that Nietzsche gives us no better reason to accept his genealogies than that they resonate with us (or some of us) psychologically or even spiritually, and at times Nietzsche is even pretty open about this. Moreover, Nietzsche's deployment of the genealogical method seems to presume that the only valid explanation of, say, Christian morality is this sort of debunking narrative.

In other words, Nietzsche's genealogy operates on the basis that there is nothing to bind us to the institution being explained other than the conditions the genealogy articulates. For example, Nietzsche seems to think that the only reason someone could believe in Christian morality is the primordial (subconscious) plot for revenge he claims to have uncovered. Nietzsche is telling us that "The Christian thinks he believes this or that, because this is the revelation of the Holy Spirit or an entailment of the absolute moral law, but the *real reason* is the primordial desire for revenge!" Christianity's claims for itself, according to Nietzsche, have been thoroughly refuted, so we must account for it in terms of some non-Christian or nonmoral just-so story. Nobody could possibly accept Christianity because it is actually true, so we go looking for a genealogical explanation of the otherwise absurd fact of the persistence of Christian belief. That, of course, begs a lot of questions!

All of that is probably enough for us to dismiss Nietzsche's genealogies as he actually executed them. Nevertheless, he has left us with a suggestion that has proven to have remarkable staying power: it seems plausible that human beings are *epistemically vulnerable*. The fact that Nietzsche's genealogies are so broadly resonate, even without much to ground them evidentially, suggests that we all do have a sneaking suspicion that we could be wrong about our own reasons for our most closely held beliefs, i.e., *we are vulnerable to put-ons!*[136] If one concludes that a Christian *might* unwittingly be a

---

[136] Even those who claim to reject Nietzsche's genealogical suggestions often fall right into employing their own genealogical subversions. If you reply to

victim of a primordial power struggle that exploits quirks in the human cognitive hardware (even if one does not conclude that this is actually the case), then one cannot help but wonder whether such vulnerabilities are indeed widespread, far beyond Christianity.

The *prima facie* plausibility of Nietzsche's genealogical method leads us to worry whether the standing of all our beliefs might be subverted by the primordial conditions under which the faculties of these beliefs were developed. Whatever one might have to say about Nietzsche's actual genealogies, he leaves us with an almost unshakeable worry that our direct sense of where our beliefs come from and what they are really doing for us might not be the only significant account to be given of the matter.

All that is merely intuitive worry, suggestion, or suspicion, which is far from having a good reason to believe we actually are subverted. Things, however, have developed quite a bit since Nietzsche wrote. We now have well-established scientific disciplines, e.g., social psychology, depth psychology, cognitive/behavioral neuroscience, branches of cognitive science, and the like, that have gone a long way toward showing that our surface sense of what we are up to is not always the real story about why we hold our beliefs, or at least it is incomplete. [137]

Of course, these disciplines are not Nietzschean in content (they are not confirming Nietzsche's just-so stories), but they are broadly genealogical in their methods. That is, the modern sciences of mind often show us that the origins of our beliefs and institutions may be found in something quite contrary to the expectations of those beliefs and institutions, and often these revelations are rather unflattering to those of us holding those expectations.[138] It's not comforting to see your most closely held picture of the world analyzed into a contrary set of categories.

Religious studies, as it is practiced in the contemporary university, is no exception to this rule, i.e, scholars of religion often account for past or

---

Nietzsche with "Sure, but you only say that about the Christian, because . . .," you are simply employing an inverted Nietzschean genealogical method. Nietzsche has a way of seducing us into an agreement, even as we try to reject him! See Malcolm Bull's fascinating *Anti-Nietzsche* (New York: Verso, 2011). Bull's proposal of "reading Nietzsche lie a loser," operating under the assumption that you are vulnerable to genealogical subversion, is essentially to any attempt to keep genealogical subversion at bay.

[137] For a good introduction to some of these issues, especially from the perspective of social psychology, see Kathleen Taylor's *Brain-Washing: The Science of Thought Control* (New York: Oxford University Press, 2017).

[138] Daniel Dennett connects Nietzschean genealogy (broadly understood) with the methodologies of many of the modern sciences of the mind in *Darwin's Dangerous Idea* (New York: Simon and Schuster, 1996).

contemporary forms of religious belief and practice in terms of (partly, at least) non-religious conditions. This or that mode of religion might be explained (to some significant degree) in terms of the environmental, biological, economic, gender, political, legal, ethnic, and/or racial conditions obtained at its origin (or maintaining it during its subsequent history).

Once again, that is not necessarily Nietzschean in content, but it is methodically genealogical. "Belief in X arose within this cultural group, because . . ." is completed not with the terms drawn from the categories of X, but the non-X conditions that have contributed to the coming to be of X. The scholar of religion will not indulge an explanation of an individual's belief ("Smith's believes X, because . . ."), and will apply her methods at higher levels of abstraction ("Belief in X arose among this cultural group, because . . .).

The fact that genealogy explains at the level of the group, but not necessarily at the level of the individual, may provide the believer with room to resist subversion while recognizing the explanatory power of the method. In any event, this shows that the religious scholar is not committed to Nietzschean subversion *per se*. Nevertheless, the scholar of religion, like all modern studies of mind, opens the possibility of our epistemic vulnerability, i.e., we are all subjected by the conditions of our primordial past to the possibility of put-ons with respect to our religious beliefs.

I am not saying that is the intent of the scholar of religion, but it is a very likely, if not inevitable, fall-out of such inquiries. Understanding ourselves comes at an expense to our naive self-confidence, because our religion's story about how and why it came to be is not necessarily the only story, or even the most authoritative story, to be told about that process.

We are, finally, ready to return to Pasulka. In the introduction to *American Cosmic*, she recounts what motivated her study of the UFO phenomenon, and it was not merely confirmatory journalism:

> When I began to focus on modern reports of UFO sightings and events, I was immediately immersed in a world where the religious impulse was alive and the formation of a new, unique form of religion was in process. I was observing it as it happened. Carl Jung put it well. Referring to the modern phenomenon of flying saucers, he wrote, "We have here a golden opportunity of seeing how a legend is formed.[139]
>
> I began to understand these individuals from the perspective of the history of religions. In a sense, they were the same cast of characters who appear at the birth of every major religious tradition, although today they have different names and job descriptions. In the first

---

[139] Pasulka, *American Cosmic*, p.10. Pasulka cites Jung, *Flying Saucers*, p. 16.

century CE they would be called scribes and redactors, but today they are agents of information, like screenwriters, television producers, and authors. I observed the dynamic genesis of a global belief system. I began to record the mechanisms by which people believe and practice, and how they believe and practice. The producers, actors, government agents, and even myself were all part of the process of the formation of belief, and perhaps even pawns in this process.[140]

What moved Pasulka was the chance to see a global religion at its genesis point. This is an opportunity to write a genealogy that is not purely speculative, but directly empirical. We cannot return to the first century CE to confirm our genealogical hunches about the coming to be of Christianity, but Pasulka can study the coming to be of the UFO religion in "real time," because this process has unfolded in our rather recent history and continues in the present moment! Pasulka then sees ufology as a religion, and she expects it to behave in its formative process like any other religion. Notice, already in these introductory remarks I quote above, we can see Pasulka's suggestion of the inherent epistemic vulnerabilities that are likely to be revealed by the genealogical investigation of the UFO religion, i.e., we might be "pawns in this process."[141]

Certainly, many mainline ufologists would not think of themselves as religious (though some do, as Pasulka points out), but that's the genealogical point—we aren't always the best judges of what is going on with our own beliefs.[142] We're vulnerable to put-ons.

---

[140] Pasulka, *American Cosmic*, pp. 10-11.

[141] If you doubt the plausibility of the claim that ufology is a burgeoning world religion, take up Pasulka's case in detail. Furthermore, suppose the origin point of the UFO religion is 1947 (Rosewell!). How plausible *prima facie* would it have been a mere seventy-five years after the life of Jesus of Nazareth to claim that Christianity would become the dominant religious system in the West? At that point some of the final drafts of the Christian Gospels might not have been completed!

[142] The fact that many (though not all) orthodox ufologists see themselves as secularists (maybe spiritual, but not religious) operating in a naturalistic scientific worldview raises interesting questions about what light Pasulka's work might shed on our understanding of secularization. In particular, there is likely a connection to be made between Pasulka's documentation of the founding of Ufology as a religion and Charles Taylor's *nova effect* thesis: "This turn has plainly altered the shape of secularity 3, namely by shifting the place of the spiritual in human life, at least as lived by many. The connection between pursuing a moral or spiritual path and belonging to larger ensembles—state, church, even denomination—has been further loosened;

Furthermore, like any other genealogical accounting, not everything Pasulka has to say about this religion's conditions of formation will be flattering, or even plausible, to the ears of its current faithful adherents. That which is epistemically dearest to us, what most forms the horizon of sense-making for our lifeworld (the picture that holds us captive), is often the hardest thing for us actually to see, let alone hold at a critical distance. Nevertheless, Pasulka is bringing the hidden or unspoken conditions of ufology into critical focus, and this process introduces the sneaking suspicion of a put-on. Indeed, Pasulka is quite clear about this possibility. At a critical juncture in *American Cosmic*, she raises considerations that are quite disturbing to the naively believing ufologist:

> The creation of a belief system is now much easier to accomplish than it was two thousand years ago, when people didn't possess smartphones and were not exposed to the ubiquitous screens of a culture that now teaches us how to see, what to see, and how to interpret what we see . . . . I was beginning to research the ways in which virtual and digital media were being used for political purposes under the auspices of information operations: how the military employed media, social media, and all types of electronic media for purposes of national security. All these media have played major roles in the creation of global belief in UFOs and extraterrestrials. It is in the world of media that the myth is created, is sustained, and proliferates.[143]

Following these remarks, Pasulka transitions into the central chapters of *American Cosmic* wherein she draws on her prior research into the cognitive science of belief formation (and the particular bearing the extended mind hypothesis has on that issue), and how these dynamics can be and probably have been used to steer belief on a mass scale. She presents the science of human cave formation. Moreover, Pasulka uses these analytical tools to operate on the popular media myths of the UFO, e.g, *Star Wars, Close*

---

and as a result the nova effect has been intensified. We're now living in a spiritual supernova, a kind of galloping pluralism on the spiritual plane" (Taylor, *A Secular Age*, (Cambridge, MA: Belknap Press, 2008), pp. 299-300). Taylor's point is that secularization is not really the West's getting over spirituality, but untying it from traditional institutions, thereby causing an explosive proliferation of spiritualities—rather than getting less religious, we're getting more religiously pluralistic. Pasulka's work on the UFO phenomenon might be seen as a snapshot of Taylor's nova effect in action.

[143] Pasulka, *American Cosmic*, pp. 82-83.

Encounters of the Third Kind, 2001: A Space Odyssey, and the *X-Files.* The picture that emerges is that ufology, as a religion, has not arisen entirely organically. It looks as though someone, or something, has co-opted popular media to steer our collective unconscious toward a particular system of belief centering on literal "nut-and-bolts" UFO technology manned by extraterrestrial, rational animals.

In short, *Pasulka's genealogy of ufology does indeed chronicle a grand-scale put-on,* and that manipulation looks like it has been transacted, at least in part, by quite mundane powers. The attentive reader of *American Cosmic* should come away with the realization that we are in the midst of a religious transformation , and this process is something that is being *done to us*—an exercise in *mass-cave formation* driven by the newly honed tools of media technology. This troubling thesis is the point of her work that remains conspicuously absent in the discussion of *American Cosmic* by mainline, i.e., *orthodox*, ufology.

Orthodox Ufology is primarily concerned with the ontological theses Pasulka advances. That, however, is not entirely surprising, because that is the typical behavior of any beleaguered orthodoxy. Once again, Nietzsche provides us great insight:

> It is a sure sign of the death of a religion when its mythic presuppositions become systematized, under the severe rational eyes of an orthodox rationalism, into a ready sum of historical events, and when people begin timidly defending the veracity of myth but at the same time resisting its natural continuance—when the feeling for myth withers and its place is taken by a religion claiming historical foundations.[144]

In other words, a sure sign that a belief system has become something akin to an orthodoxy is when its sustenance depends on empirical-historical verification. Nietzsche marks this need for confirmation as a sign of the death of a religion, but maybe it is also the sign of its origination too—the establishment of a religion, no less than its holding on past its time, requires an ontical, historical foothold.

In any event, Nietzsche gives us the plausible suggestion that there is something importantly common between Orthodox Ufology and any of the fundamentalist forms of traditional religion, i.e., an insistence on the literal truth of the minutiae of their founding beliefs. This fundamentalist picture of the UFO is then what holds the Orthodox Ufologist captive, and he or she thereby misses the therapeutic effect that Pasulka's *partially* subverting

---

[144] Nietzsche, *The Birth of Tragedy,* trans Francis Golffing (New York: Anchor Books, 1956), p. 68.

genealogy might have provided. The "partially" in my previous sentence is crucial, because this is what separates Pasulka's genealogies (and those of many other religious scholars) from outright Nietzschean debunking.[145]

Pasulka is clear about her UFO realism, i.e, she is convinced there is something real operating behind or through the experience of what the Orthodox Ufologist calls "the UFO." Unlike Nietzsche, Pasulka does not begin with the presumption that the religious believer is suffering from a sort of inherited cognitive deception.[146] There is a core, experiential truth at the origin point of ufology. Consider the following:

> These "contact events," the perceived interface between the human and the intelligent non-human being from the sky, spawn beliefs and interpretations. These beliefs and interpretations develop into communities of belief, or faith communities . . . . Similar to religions, institutions, cultivate, and sometimes intervene in the interpretations of a UFO event. These institutions vary and range from religious institutions to governments to clubs or groups, and, today, to social media groups.[147]

Thus, religious origins are two-pronged: *originating experience* followed by *interpretive memory*. On the one hand, SOMETHING shows up in the presence of humans that demands an interpretation, even though it is utterly

---

[145] Note that Orthodox Ufology has been blind to this message for decades. For example, in *The Invisible College*, Jacques Vallée claims, regarding the cultural effect of the the the UFO phenomenon, "We are not here dealing with escapism — we are dealing with the next form of religion." Moreover, in his somewhat later writings (*Messengers of Deception* and *Revelations*), Vallée is increasingly open that he suspects that this belief formation is not only being done by the phenomenon, but to a high degree by mundane powers with the ability to manipulate the popular imagination, and Pasulka notes this in *American Cosmic*. We can find similar concerns in John Keel's *Operation Trojan Horse*. Vallée's and Keel's thinking on this issue remains quite opaque and inchoate, and it isn't until *American Cosmic* that we get a full application of the tools available to contemporary academia to this aspect of the phenomenon. In any event, there have been Nietzschean genealogical suspicions circling around Ufology for quite a while.

[146] In *American Cosmic*, Pasulka is quite open about her own religious practice. She is clearly not out to further the Nietzschean subversion of religion. See *American Cosmic*, pp. 87-88 and pp. 223-224. To be fair, Nietzsche has moments in some of his works that are far less dismissive of religious experience, as opposed to religion.

[147] Pasulka, *American Cosmic*, p, 12.

novel relative to our common experience. On the other hand, all that the human being has at her disposal to construct this interpretation of the originating experience is the set of categories she has inherited at that historically contingent time and place.

On this point, i.e., the two-pronged nature of religion, Pasulka seems to be an important figure in a movement of religion scholars who are trying to diffuse the tired dichotomy between reductively constructivist accounts of religion ("It's all *just* a put on!") and naive realism about religious claims ("Creation must have happened in exactly six days!"). For example, in the paragraph I have just introduced, Pasulka quotes the following remarks from Jeff Kripal: "Some of the remembered effects of these fantastic states of mind have been taken up by extremely elaborate social, political, and artistic processes and have been fashioned by communities into mythical, ritual, and institutional complexes that have fundamentally changed human history. We call these 'religions'."[148]

We need to remember this EVENT, but we can only do so in the terms we have in our current vocabulary, which never really fit; they weren't "designed" to deal with this kind of experience.[149] Thus, the interpretation is subject to falling into a put-on, and maybe that is even an inevitability. In this way, all religion is a sort of put-on in a benign sense: we are *putting on* a bit of theater to try to get at a *reality* we cannot fully and explicitly articulate.

This is the source of our epistemic vulnerability—religious experience forces us to apply our ordinary categories of sense-making beyond their proper scope, and that leaves us ripe for manipulation (*put-ons* in a malignant sense). Nevertheless, Pasulka, and those of her school of religious studies, do not doubt that the originating experience is real. *The original event of the "divine" showing up on the margins of our cave is no put-on!*

---

[148] Kripal and Strieber, *The Super Natural: A New Vision of the Unexpected*, pp. 5-6. See also Kripal's *Superhumanities*. I make a case that this approach is something close akin to how Aristotle thought about religious mythology in chapter 2 above.

[149] Employing a common philosophical distinction, we might say that the terms in our interpretive memory get things right in their *reference* (they refer us back to the originating experience of the EVENT), even though their *sense* may miss the mark. Bernardo Kastrup develops something akin to this view in his *More Than Allegory: On Religious Myth, Truth, and Belief* (New York: IFF Books, 2016). Moreover, this approach is not entirely foreign even to some stands of orthodox Catholic theology. For example, something along these lines might be seen in Ratzinger's discussion of the Trinity in *Introduction to Christianity* (San Francisco, CA: Ignatius Press, 2003), though I'm sure that claim is controversial among his interpreters!

Thus, Pasulka is not saying, *a la* Nietzsche speaking to the Christian, "You're just one more fool duped by your own history!" No, Pasulka does not discount the reality that occasions what the UFO believer holds dear, nor does she do so regarding any religious experience. She does, however, caution the UFO believer that he or she, as a human, is subject to epistemic vulnerabilities, especially now that there are many among us willing and able to exploit those all-too-human weaknesses. We are natural cave dwellers, and our current technological situation leaves us more vulnerable to *put-ons* than ever before in our history, so we need to have a steadfast wariness in our approach to religions currently coming "online."

I think Pauslka's point then goes far beyond an attempt to exorcize the picture captivating the Orthodox Ufologist. She has something to show all religious believers, which is to say all humans (like it or not!), and I hope that this is what my student will learn from my answer to her question. We can ask dark questions about our most closely cherished beliefs, admitting that they might be, to some degree, put-ons. That is merely to admit the epistemic vulnerability of the human condition. This admission of epistemic vulnerability, however, is far from conceding that our beliefs are *just* put-ons, for they are occasioned by the experience of something real, memories of something uncanny that really did show up here. Keep in mind the Platonic notion we discussed in chapter 1 that memory is our only access to what we experience outside our caves. If we can free ourselves from too constrictive pictures (interpretations) of those originating experiences, we may encounter anew the saving powers that reach out to us; we might remember.

This is the most enticing suggestion that I hear in my reading of *American Cosmic.* My students, who are mostly traditionally minded Christians, are actually fairly comfortable with the suggestion of epistemic vulnerability. The picture holding them captive has been under genealogical pressure at least since Nietzsche first developed the method, and they are aware of the critique. Thus, I believe they are ultimately well disposed to understand Pasulka's message. I hope that this will eventually become the case for those religious believers for whom her message is most directly pertinent.

7 Apocalyptic Philosophizing:
Jacques Vallée as the Oppenheimer of the Digital Age

"At first, they saw but seeing was no use;
they heard but didn't hear. Like shapes in dream,
they passed long lives in purposeless confusion. . . .
And I did more for them.
I invented number, cleverest of devices,
and writing, hard at work to help recall
all things to memory, the Muses' mother. . . .
I found all these contrivances for mortals,
But to my sorrow I have no device
By which to escape my present misery."

—Aeschylus, *Prometheus Bound*[150]

"As an empiricist I continue to think of the conceptual scheme of science as a tool, ultimately, for predicting future experience in the light of past experience. Physical objects are conceptually imported into the situation as convenient intermediaries - not by definition in terms of experience, but simply as irreducible posits comparable, epistemologically, to the gods of Homer."

—W.V.O. Quine, *Two Dogmas of Empiricism*[151]

---

[150] Aeschylus, *Prometheus Bound*, trans Deborah Roberts (Indianapolis, IN: Hackett, 2012), 460-485.
[151] W.V.O. Quine, "Two Dogmas of Empiricism," in *From Logical Point of View* (Cambridge, MA: Harvard University Press, 1980), §6.

"We're already dealing with an alien intelligence in our own emails, ChatGPT et cetera. We don't know what it's doing, so imagine if you were a million years ahead of us—how do you have a dialogue with something like that?"

—Gary Nolan[152]

"But deities and supernatural characters do not exist in the ways in which we assumed they existed."

—Diana Pasulka, *Encounters*[153]

In her preface to *American Cosmic*, Diana Pasulka claims that "If Jacques were an essay, he would be 'The Question Concerning Technology' by the philosopher Martin Heidegger."[154] In a draft version of that preface, she explains this claim by contrasting two readings of Heidegger's essay:

> There are two ways to interpret Heidegger's essay. One way is to place technology within a much-invoked mythological tradition whereby it is associated with the sacred. This tradition is best exemplified by the myth of the Greek titan Prometheus, who delivers technology, *techne*, to humans but is punished for it by the Greek gods. It must be a terrible crime, as Prometheus's punishment is to be forever chained to a rock with his stomach exposed to the elements. During each afternoon, an eagle eats his liver, which regenerates at night, only to be eaten again the next day by another eagle. The latest manifestation of the mythos of technology as a gift from the heavens occurs in UFO folklore, wherein the gods become non-humans.[155]

---

[152] Gary Nolan, quoted in "Stanford Professor Says Aliens are 100% on Earth, US Is Reverse-Engineering UFOs':: https://www.news.com.au/technology/science/space/stanford-professor-says-aliens-are-100-per-cent-on-earth-us-is-reverseengineering-downed-ufos/news-story/041694ef5df4791fbdfa303a08f34a9c. Accessed May 22, 2023.

[153] Diana Pasulka, *Encounters: Experiences with Nonhuman Intelligences* (St. Martin's: New York, 2023), p. 99.

[154] Diana Pasulka, *American Cosmic: UFOs, Religion, Technology* (New York: Oxford University Press, 2019), p. xii.

[155] Diana Pasulka, "A Tour of Silicon Valley with Jacques Vallée," Draft: https://www.academia.edu/34657465/A_Tour_of_Silicon_Valley_with_Jacques_Vallée (accessed 5/15/23), p. 9-10.

On this reading, Heidegger's point would be that technology is something like a foreign power that was given to humanity from a great beyond, e.g. the Titan Prometheus or devil in the prelapsarian garden. The introduction of technology, which, according to the Promethean story, is the creation of distinctive humanity itself, requires something like a supernatural or miraculous intervention. As Pasulka puts it, "In all cases the myth articulates the idea that technology is not generated by humans but is somehow derived supernaturally, as a gift from either gods or non-humans."[156] This intervention, carries game-changing consequences in terms of human power, and that's why Zeus (ever-protective of the dominion of gods over humanity) issues the sternest possible punishment to Prometheus; technology is the source of intractable human power, and therefore a threat to the very notion of divinity.[157]

If we apply this reading of Heidegger to the UFO phenomenon, then "found artifacts from crashed extraterrestrial or non-human craft have been reverse-engineered to produce modern technologies that appear to be almost supernatural, like mind-reading computers and computer-human interfaces."[158] The extraterrestrials or ultraterrestrials that gave us the original technological insights are the real, demythologized sources of our subsequent development. Heidegger's essay is rather gloomy about our current technological situation, and that makes some sense of this Promethean reading: the gods competing with our Promethean progenitors are not impressed with our grasping of their fire, and we are running headlong into our long overdue comeuppance. The point is that humans have gotten their hands on things that maybe we shouldn't have, through the intervention of gods or aliens understood in the terms of our Goldilocks Ontology. Heidegger would then be taken as giving us a cautionary tale about the coming punishment.[159]

Notice how this reading of Heidegger, as applied to the UFO, fits comfortably with the sort of Ufology fundamentalism I put into question in the last chapter. It's part of the equivalent of six-day creationism in the theology of UFOism. Pasulka is correct that this reading of Heidegger (and application to the UFO phenomenon) is only available "upon first inspection"

---

[156] Pasulka, "A Tour of Silicon Valley with Jacques Vallée," p. 10.

[157] Milton based his version of Satan in *Paradise Lost* on Prometheus, and certainly Shelly has this view of humanity getting out of hand in *Frankenstein*.

[158] Pasulka, "A Tour of Silicon Valley with Jacques Vallée," p. 10.

[159] It is always interesting to note how much of Ufology, while rejecting traditional religious authority and affirming an Enlightenment story of secularization, adopts or unconsciously reiterates the same archetypical structure of spiritual warfare that we find in the classical Abrahamic faiths.

and when the essay is "not read carefully"[160], and it results in an equally pedestrian application to the UFO.

Pasulka contrasts this Promethean interpretation of "The Question Concerning Technology" with

> another sense in which Heidegger's essay can be read. At its most radical, understanding the essence of technology involves a form of mystical engagement. Mysticism, in this sense, is not a fixation, as Heidegger noted, "on sentences and topics," but involves a relationship with and to something. A relationship implies a process, something alive, not dead or static. Heidegger's essay challenges its readers to leave aside the view of technology as an instrument and as mythological or mysteriously formed, but asks its readers instead to grasp technology's import and influence—which is why his essay reminds me of Jacques Vallée.[161]

On this reading, which is most certainly central to what Heidegger was really doing, technology is not understood in terms of just the devices we use to structure or manipulate our environment, but as a way of *being-in-the-world*, an implicit attitude or cognitive background that frames all of our explicit understandings of things. For Heidegger, technology is not a collection of beings we happen to have possessed or mastered, but an attitude toward Being, which partly determines the beings to which we attuned, (as opposed to other possibilities for what garner our attention).

In the terminology we have been employing throughout this book, technology is the basic *cognitive* principle that forms our going *Umwelt*, everydayness, or cave. In recent centuries (and even more so in recent decades) we have endured a series of technological innovations unprecedented in our history, at least in terms of the speed with which these changes have become ubiquitous within the structure of our experience. Once again, it's not new technological devices but new technological attitudes toward the world, or an intensification of those attitudes, that marks our new era. Our world, though always technological, is on the move at an unprecedented scale, and this is the important connection Pasulka sees between Vallée and Heidegger:

> Jacques is fully aware of the revolution that is technology. Although he had most likely never read the essay, Jacques's description of France as a dead society and Silicon Valley as the home of the new

---

[160] "A Tour of Silicon Valley with Jacques Vallée," p. 10.
[161] "A Tour of Silicon Valley with Jacques Vallée," p. 10.

resonates with Heidegger's assessment of technology as a new era of human experience that was framing a brand new epoch.[162]

Like Heidegger, Vallée understands both that humanity is inherently technological and we have pushed this way of being to a novel level of complexity, danger, and, maybe, hope.

I believe Pasulka is correct in her preferred reading of Heidegger and the connection she makes between "The Question Concerning Technology" and Vallée. Notice, too, that Pasulka begins *American Cosmic* by suggesting this Heideggarian connection with Vallée and ends that same text leaving us to ruminate on a quotation from Heidegger, "Only a God can save us."[163] Obviously, she is giving us a clue to the deeply Heideggarian theme of the book; Heidegger is where she begins and she brings us full circle back to his thought as she ends her reflection. Heidegger gets the first and last words in *American Cosmic*. Like the clear Nietzschean themes Pasulka evokes throughout the body of *American Cosmic*, the Heideggarian "book-ending" of her project in her preface and conclusion has largely gone unnoticed by Ufology, much to the detriment of how well this line of argument has been understood within that community.

Where any attention to these sorts of themes is mustered, it mostly operates at the level of the superficial Promethean literalism I mentioned above. More grist for the orthodox Ufologist mill: "The aliens have given us this great gift of technology, which is what will either doom or save us from ourselves!" As such, much as I tried to do so for the Nietzschean piece of *American Cosmic* in the previous chapter, I am going to attempt to make the *sophisticated* Heideggarian contribution to our understanding of the UFO a bit more explicit. Thus, what follows should be taken to a large extent as an elaboration of what is implicit in Pasulka's thought, or at least she opens these pathways to us. I am not necessarily claiming that these are pathways Pasulka herself would care to follow; except for her opening and closing remarks, Heidegger is mostly an unspoken presence in *American Cosmic*. Be that as it may, Pasulka's introduction of Heidegger into the discourse about ufology has made fruitful avenues of thought available to us, and I am going to travel a few of them in this chapter. Moreover, I am going to make a case that there is a sophisticated version of the Promethean vision that we should bring to bear on these considerations. For now, however, we must start by getting on with the hard work of understating Heidegger's nearly opaque essay.

There is no really good place to start on "The Question Concerning Technology," so I begin simply by putting some texts into play that will help

---

[162] "A Tour of Silicon Valley with Jacques Vallée," p. 10.

[163] Pasulka, *American Cosmic*, p. 244.

us understand how Heidegger poses this question in his own (frustratingly!) novel way:

> Technology is not equivalent to the essence of technology. . . . That which pervades every tree, as tree, is not itself a tree that can be counted among all the other trees.[164]

> Everywhere we remain unfree and chained to technology, whether we passionately affirm or deny it. But we are delivered over to it as something neutral; for this conception of it, to which we particularly like to do homage, makes us utterly blind to the essence of technology." (QT, p. 4)

> If we inquire, step by step, into what technology, represented as means, actually is, then we shall arrive at revealing. The possibility of all productive manufacturing lies in revealing (QT, p. 12)

> Technology is no mere means. Technology is a way of revealing. (QT, p. 12)

In these remarks, Heidegger is trying to disabuse us of our default tendency to think of technology solely in terms of the devices and social organizations. (Remember that bureaucracies and other sorts of rational social institutions are human inventions.) This view is what Heidegger has in mind when he mentions taking technology as "something neutral" or "represented as means." Under the influence of this "common sense" view of technology, we say things like "My iPhone is neither good nor bad, it just depends on what I do with it," "There is nothing wrong with meticulous urban planning, as long as it is done fairly," or "nuclear power is not inherently evil, because it can be used for both production and destruction."

Heidegger is not denying that such statements are true, but he does claim that our failure to see a deeper essence of technology is partly why "we remain unfree and chained to technology." That is, by exclusively thinking of technology in terms of devices or specific methods of social organization, we miss a more profound question and graver consequences that follow from how we answer it. This deeper and more threatening essence of technology is what Heidegger wants to call our attention to the "The Question Concerning Technology."

---

[164] Martin Heidegger, "The Question Concerning Technology," in *The Question Concerning Technology and Other Essays*, trans William Levitt (New York: Harper, 1977), p.4. Further references of this essay will be given parenthetically as "QT" followed by the page number.

Moreover, in Heidegger's view, thinking of the essence of technology as a neutral means to various ends is superficial. As he argues elsewhere:

> Modern technology is not constituted by, and does not consist in, the installation of electric motors and turbines and similar machinery; that sort of thing can on the contrary be erected only to the extent to which the essence of technology has already assumed dominion. Our age is not a technological age because it is the age of the machine; it is an age of the machine because it is the technological age. But so long as the essence of technology does not closely concern us, in our thought, we shall never be able to know what the machine is.[165]

That is, our devices and social organizations are *our productions, we make them*. If we have a suspicion that these means have gotten us into trouble, that raises the question of why we got in the business of making such things in the first place. Why we initiated the technological age and what this implies about us and our understanding of Being are the deeper targets of Heidegger's questioning. What does technology implicate about us such that we have produced all these entities that can be used for good or *ill*? Why have we put ourselves in a situation wherein we are faced with the possibility of ruining our capacity for focused attention, the forfeiture of our personal freedoms, and maybe species-wide extinction by instrumentalities we have introduced into our environment? What is going on in our background such that we are bringing these devices and contrivances, with which we are undeniably obsessed, into our foreground? Why have we filled our lives (both literally and spatially in terms of our concerns) with these devices? These are the questions concerning technology that Heidegger believes our ordinary queries ignore, all-too conveniently.

As you can see above, Heidegger claims that this deeper essence of technology is a *revealing*. The technological way of *being-in-the-world*, like any other fundamental attitude, sorts the world for us in terms of relevance. As we have discussed from the beginning of the book, human cognition works by narrowing the indefinite possibilities for experience and action down to a manageable set of beings based on their relevance to our projects and histories. These basic attitudes *reveal* to us certain entities out the whirl of what is out there. Our implicit understanding is what lets something come into the light for us, while leaving other things in the background.

Moreover, as we also discussed, part of the way humans do this business of revealing is by making things on which we can off-load our burdens, cognitive and non-cognitive. Thus, there is a sense in which our

---

[165] Martin Heidegger, *What is Called Thinking?* trans. Glenn Gray (New York: Harper, 1976), p. 24.

implicit understandings and practices have revealed a world to us. Heidegger believes that *our* basic stance, which reveals a world of entities to us, is technology. Our basic attitudes that form our way of *being-in-the-world* not only reveal entities for us, but they also say something about us, i.e., *they reveal what it is that we most care about in our encounter with the world.* In other words, a world is revealed to us by our interpretation of Being, what it means to be at all, so how we reveal the world then tells us a great deal about ourselves and what we most value.

What, we might ask, does Heidegger think is importantly different about the *modern technological* way of sorting the world, and what does that reveal about us? According to Heidegger, "The revealing that rules modern technology is a "challenging", which puts to nature unreasonable demands that it is to "supply energy that can be extracted and stored as such." (QT, p. 14). That is, we have come to be primarily concerned with what we can manage, manipulate, store, and expend, and the entities that we thus encounter in our cave are those most submissive to our ends. Thus, for us "The world now appears as an object open to the attacks of calculative thought, attacks that nothing is believed able any longer to resist. Nature becomes a gigantic gasoline station, an energy source for modern technology and industry."[166] Thus, our fundamental concern is over what we can manage and control, so what we primarily see is what we can manage and control. We transform the world into a great conglomeration of manipulative devices because the structuring principle of our thinking is control and manipulation (Heidegger's "calculative thinking"). For us, Being is to be a "standing reserve" for consumption. We then experience nature primarily in terms of its potential for such extraction and consumption.

Heidegger believes that this has not always been the case for us, and our mixing ourselves with the environment, and the implicit assumptions according to which we have done so, have been importantly different:

> The hydroelectric plant is not built into the Rhine River as was the old wooden bridge that joined bank with bank for hundreds of years. Rather the river is dammed up into the power plant. What the river is now, namely, a waterpower supplier, derives from the essence of the power station. In order that we may even remotely consider the monstrousness that reigns here, let us ponder for a moment the contrast that speaks out of the two titles, "The Rhine" as dammed up into the *power* works, and "The Rhine" as uttered out of the *art* work . . . . But, it will be replied, the Rhine is still a river in the landscape, is it not? Perhaps. But how? In no other way than as an object on call for

---

[166] Martin Heidegger, "Memorial Address," in *Discourse on Thinking*, trans J. Anderson and E. Freund (New York: Harper, 1966), p. 50.

inspection by a tour group ordered there by the vacation industry. (QT, p. 16)

Heidegger's point is that our ancestors dealt with a river by building around it and with it in a way that met human ends in accord with the natural environment as we encountered it, and likely religious and cultural rituals would have sprung up to sacralize this accord, e.g., the bridge would be consecrated to a saint or god of the river in gratitude for working with us. The wooden bridge over the river met nature on its own terms. The modern hydro-electric dam and the industry of tourism and curiosity, however, take the river as a resource to be exploited (energy to be extracted and stored), which is interesting to us only if it exists on our terms of use. The more ancient attitude was to see us as working in tandem with nature, whereas now we can only see things in terms of how they are *accessible to us*.[167] We have become domineering narcissists on a grand scale: we define the world in terms of its accessibility to us, and then force it to live according to our demands. For Heidegger, our modern technological attitude is an interpretation of Being as that which is *here for us*. It is the height of humanistic hubris.

Certainly, Heidegger is worried about the possibility of environmental disaster, our ever-diminishing capacity to resist distraction (to think!), and even nuclear Armageddon, but these are not the greatest dangers inherent in the essence of technology: "an attack with technological means is being prepared upon the life and nature of man compared with which the explosion the hydrogen bomb means very little. For precisely if the hydrogen bomb does *not* explode and human life on earth is preserved, an uncanny change in the world moves upon us."[168]

That is big talk, especially as we seem to have recently rekindled the dark possibility of a nuclear holocaust (or maybe just reminded ourselves of it), but remember that Heidegger wrote those words with a straight face will sitting at ground zero for the most tense moments of the first run of the Cold War. What then is the greatest danger? Heidegger spells it out in two different ways, but we can see that they are internally related. First, even if we do not literally destroy ourselves (and much else!) through environmental degradation or nuclear warfare, *we will in some sense be consumed by our technological creations:*

> If man is challenged, ordered, to do this, then does not man himself belong even more originally than nature within the standing reserve? The current talk about human resources, about the supply of patients for the clinic, gives evidence of this. The forester who, in the wood,

---

[167] This juxtaposition can already be seen in Plato's cautionary myth pitting primordial Athens against Atlantis in his underappreciated dialogue *Critias*.
[168] Heidegger, "The Memorial Address," p. 52. Heidegger's emphasis.

measures the felled timber and to all appearances walks the same forest path in the same way as did his grandfather is today commanded by profit-making in the lumber industry . . . made subordinate to the orderability of cellulose, which for its part challenged forth by the need for paper, which is then delivered to newspapers and illustrated magazines. The latter, in their turn, set public opinion to swallowing what is printed, so that a set configuration of opinion becomes available on demand. (QT, p. 18)

As soon as what is unconcealed no longer concerns man even as object, but does so, rather, exclusively as standing-reserve, and man in the midst of objectlessness is nothing but the orderer of the standing-reserve, then he comes to the very brink of a precipitous fall; that is, he comes to the point where he himself will have to be taken as standing reserve. (QT, p. 27)

Heidegger's point here is that our insistence on revealing a world in terms of its orderability to our demands, its accessibility to us, will inevitably be applied to us. We will see ourselves as no different from the mass of nature that we have reductively defined in terms of its pliability for our consumption. We are part of that same natural "order," so we can expect that we will eventually treat ourselves as just one more resource to be fed into our machines. That certainly is a strike against our dignity, and we probably don't (or shouldn't) need to be reminded of the high body count that has come with the notion of disposable and consumable humanity over the last century or so. Once again, Heidegger doesn't necessarily have those starkly mortal possibilities in mind (though he doesn't deny them either), and his concern is with more mundane concerns that undermine our sense of distinctively human worth. Note his examples of "human resources," "the supply of patients," the lumberjack whose work has been reduced to mere mechanical compliance, and our subjugation to a media system bent on manufacturing opinion. In all these cases, what is most tenderly and intimately humane (our work, our health, our thoughts) is being replaced by the mechanism of technical processes that might as well be fulfilled by non-human hardware. The lumberjack, no different from the wood he cuts, is just so much pulp being prepared for consumption. We humans, or that about us that is distinctively human, become bugs and not features of the process: "Man must have nothing to perform in the course of technical operations; after all, he is the source of error," so "Eliminate the individual [human], and excellent results ensue."[169]

This notion of a human disposability and subsequent mechanical

---

[169] Jacques Ellul, *The Technological Society*, trans John Wilkinson (New YorkVintage, 1964), p. 136.

obsolescence is a theme pursued acutely by one of Heidegger's most underappreciated students, Gunther Anders: "Viewed from the perspective of institutions, the economy, the leisure industry, politics, and warfare—all of which make use of us as instruments of labor, consumers, or victims of some other kind—this replaceability is already an undeniable fact"[170] Anders' point is that we no longer seem integral to the processes we have unleashed. Our economy, media (news and entertainment, supposing those can be distinguished), politics, and warfare are close to being able to get on rather well without much input from us. We are becoming ancillary to, and maybe even a drag on, these processes, which now operate almost autonomously from any distinctively human thinking or decision making. We are disposable parts in the mechanized process, and maybe our value in even that role is now short-lived.

Crucially for our discussion below, Anders identifies the advent of human obsolescence with the development and use of the first nuclear weapons. What strikes Anders in particular about the creation of the bomb is that nobody seems to bear any sense of personal guilt or a troubled conscience over participating in the introduction of the most horrific weapon in human history. Anders believes that the lack of personal guilt stems from the fact that "the monstrous undertaking... is not carried out by individuals, but by a complex and vastly ramified organization."[171] That is, the creation and use of the bomb was as much something that *happened to* the people involved in the process as it was something *they did*. Individual human agency was not the prime mover behind the project. Nobody bears personal guilt because nobody really had control over the process; everyone was just a disposable part operating in a vastly incomprehensible whole. As Anders puts it:

> We are here beyond both morality and immorality. To blame the participants for their lack of conscience would be as meaningless as to ascribe courage or cowardice to one's hand. Just as a mere hand cannot be cowardly, so a mere participant cannot have conscience. The division of labor prevents him from having a clear insight into the productive process, that lack of conscience we must ascribe to him is no longer an individual deficiency.[172]

---

[170] Gunther Anders, "Promethean Shame," in *Promethean Shame: Technology, Digital Culture, and Human Obsolescence*, tans Christopher John Miller (New York: Rowan & Littlefield 2016), p. 55. Miller's commentary in this volume is indispensable.

[171] Gunther Anders, "Reflections on the H-Bomb," *Dissent* (Spring 1956), p. 150.

[172] Anders, "Reflections on the H-Bomb," p. 150.

A machine is "beyond good and evil," and therefore it is not troubled by the hindrances of conscience. Inasmuch as we have been incorporated into our machines, i.e., *we* don't run things anymore, our moral qualms simply don't arise. It's not a question of whether *we* should be doing this, *we* aren't the ones doing it. We bear no more responsibility for what "our" machines do than my left foot bears for my running a race. Since machines are not responsible individuals, and we have been reduced to mechanical parts, then nobody really has responsibility. In a mechanized world, conscience is obsolete.

In light of our discussion in earlier chapters, we can see that Anders takes a process like the development and use of the bomb as something like a hyperobject. The Manhattan Project, though it was initiated by human beings, took on a life of its own at a level beyond human control or even comprehension. Did we really know *what we were doing* or *what we had done?* For Anders, *we* didn't do it; the Manhattan Project did it. We were not running the Manhattan Project, but it ran us, as it took on a scale that dwarfs our ordinary modes of thinking. The Manhattan Project existed (still exists?) mostly in our *Uber-Umwelt*, so we only glimpse it at the margins. The Manhattan Project, as a hyperobject, confronts us as a vastly superior *alien* Other. Anders makes this inversion clear as follows:

> The Promethean dream of omnipotence has at long last come true though in an unexpected form . . . . we are no longer today what men have called "men." Although we are unchanged anatomically, our completely changed relation to the cosmos and ourselves had transformed us into a new species—beings that differ from the previous type of man no less than Nietzsche's superman differed from man. In other words—and this is not meant as mere metaphor—we are Titans at least as long as we are omnipotent without making *definitive* use of this omnipotence of ours.[173]

You might be thinking something like "Didn't Truman have his hands on the reins?" or "Wasn't Oppenheimer running the Manhattan Project?" Fair enough, but one wonders whether even these twentieth century Titans had a grasp of the full scope and complexity of what they were doing, especially when we think of the Manhattan Project as just a fingertip of the undeniable hyperobject that was (is?) World War II. Given the mechanistic logic of industrialized death production that had taken over the world in the war, how much choice did Truman really have?

Moreover, remember Oppenheimer's famous quotation from the *Bhagavad-Gita* as he watched the test at Trinity: "Now I am become death, the destroyer of worlds." Fine, but then why have you done this? Oppenheimer

---

[173] Anders, "Reflections on the H-Bomb," p. 146.

seems to have believed that the bomb was inevitable. Technology was out of his control. He, as a scientist and engineer, is merely the expression of this greater force running by its own inexorable logic. Oppenheimer, like everybody else, was taken up into a hyperobject, which we can hardly understand. At that point, an alien presence was already on the scene and exerting irresistible influence over us.

Prometheus has fulfilled his promise and made us omnipotent Titans with the power to destroy our world. Remember, however, at least by Aeschylus's accounting, Hephaestus goes out of his way to point out to Prometheus that he is chained to the rock of his torture by a piece of technology:

> Here, now, display your arrogance and steal
> gods' privileges for creatures of a day.
> How can mortals lessen this suffering?
> The gods call you Prometheus, Forethinker:
> false name. You lack the forethought you require
> to twist your way out of *this work of art*.[174]

Prometheus is a tragic figure, and his children are likewise in for bitter irony. The very source of our godlike status is likewise what will ultimately bind us, like Prometheus, to a rock by our devices. Our great liberation from the Gods, the Promethean fire, ultimately binds us to an even more domineering master. As Anders puts it, not only are we the first Titans to walk the earth (as far as we know), but likewise "the first dwarfs . . . who are granted survival only to further orders."[175]

In short, our Promethean pretensions have given us vast power, but they simultaneously leave us at the mercy of a superior being at whose behest we now serve. Heidegger's gloomy worries over our being overtaken by our own technological mentality are much more than nostalgia for the good old days. For Anders, the coming moment of Promethean irony "may result in the death of all mankind"[176], and I believe he means that both literally (nuclear annihilation) and more broadly as the end of anything distinctively human in subjugation to a mechanical hyperobject.

Moreover, today with the seemingly autonomous operation of AI, social media, and vast techniques of social organization and domination, we are being overtaken by many "gods" whose inception was in our insistence on revealing the world in terms of its accessibility to our whims and needs. For the Heideggarian cast of mind, the inevitably ironic rebounding of our

---

[174] Aeschylus, *Prometheus Bound*, 85-90.

[175] Quoted in Miller's commentary in *Promethean Shame*, p. 112.

[176] Anders, "Reflections on the H-Bomb," p. 150.

attempts at control into our subjugation is the bitter tragedy of all unchecked humanism.

Not everyone in the history of thinking has seen the Promethean bargain as lamentable, even when it is understood as the ultimate overcoming of humanity. As Friedrich Nietzsche puts it: "In the long run, it is not a question of man at all: he is to be overcome."[177] Nietzsche's view is that humanity's natural condition is unredeemed suffering because of our self-consciousness. We are tormented not only by the bodily ailments and inevitable mortality of all living beings, but further by the need to find some meaning or justification for these travails. Thus, humanity mystifies and tortures itself even more with fantasies about good and evil as a means to justify our struggles.

Now, however, Nietzsche believes that we are finally able to get beyond all those torments by creating a "higher form of being," a super-man, who is not subject to worries over the meaning of its existence. Nietzsche has various versions of the super-man, but the one relevant to our discussion has a technological flair.[178] On this view, the super-man will come:

> Once we possess that common economic management of the earth that will soon be inevitable, mankind will be able to find its best meaning as a machine in the service of this economy—as a tremendous clockwork, composed of ever smaller, ever more subtly "adapted" gears; as an ever-growing superfluity of all dominating and commanding elements; as a whole of tremendous force, whose individual factors represent minimal forces, minimal values.[179]

> The task is to make man as useful as possible and to approximate him, as far as possible, to an infallible machine: to this end he must be

---

[177] Friedrich Nietzsche, *The Will to Power*, trans Walter Kaufmann and R.J. Hollingdale (New York: Random House, 1967), §440

[178] For an in-depth treatment of Nietzsche's other versions of the super-man, see Paul S. Loeb, *The Death of Nietzsche's Zarathustra* (New York: Cambridge University Press, 2012). Jeff Kripal makes very good use of Loeb's reading of Nietzsche in *Superhumanities*. The version of the super-man I am presenting is almost certainly not Nietzsche's most considered view; it's based almost entirely on just a few passages from *Will to Power*, which is itself somewhat suspect as representative of Nietzsche's preferred views. Heidegger, whose thought is my main aim in this chapter, however, reads Nietzsche through the lens of *Will to Power*, and he mainly critiques Nietzsche as the most technological thinker. See Heidegger's "The Word of Nietzsche 'God is Dead," in *The Question Concerning Technology and Other Essays*, 53–114.

[179] Nietzsche, *Will to Power*, §866

equipped with the virtues of the machine — he must learn to experience states in which he works in a mechanically useful way as the supremely valuable states; hence it is necessary to spoil other states for him as much as possible, as highly dangerous and disreputable.[180]

By becoming as machine-like as possible, or even raw materials for machine consumption, Nietzsche believes we can finally be free of both the unredeemable suffering of our cognizance of the meaninglessness of existence and the burden of the ideals that are supposed to be its remedy. Machines do not suffer, and they are not tempted to indulge quixotic fantasies about the meaning and possible dignity of their existence. We are not machines, primarily because we are concerned, and giving a damn about ourselves, and our shared world comes at a cost in consternation.

Nietzsche, at least as he expresses his vision in the passages I have cited immediately above, sees the mechanization of humanity at its own hands as the beginning of an evolutionary stage that will culminate in a being who is liberated from the burden of caring, who can operate with complete mechanical efficiency in an endless assertion of power. By becoming cogs in a great machine, Nietzsche does not see a descent to the subhuman, but an ascent to the super-human. The machine is the unconstrained and unconscious expression of power—the ultimate coincidence of Being and the will to power. Nietzsche envisions a super-man as a sort of technological hyperobject.

His vision is transhumanist: humanity will be subsumed into a mechanically administered collective unconsciousness. This is not to say that Nietzsche has in mind literal cyborgs or our complete replacement by intelligent robots we (or some among us) have designed. Maybe, but it's also as likely that Nietzsche's vision is a good bit subtler. In the passage I cite above, Nietzsche points to the necessity of getting people habituated into the "virtues of the machine" in order to bring about the great overcoming. That is, the human being must grow accustomed to and well-disposed toward a merely mechanical state of existence; we must become inured to being subject to a mechanical control mechanism. We will learn to prefer a psychological or spiritual mechanism over other non-mechanical possibilities for being. This End of Things will be brought about not by a genocidal attack by robots or nuclear annihilation, but by our collective forgetting what makes us distinctively human (our distinctively human self-consciousness with all its pains and joys), leaving us ripe for mechanical domination.

The apocalypse will come by the slow habituation of humanity into the inhuman, which for Nietzsche is super-human. According to this vision,

---

[180] Nietzsche, *Will to Power*, §888

the world indeed ends "Not with a bang, but a whimper" whereby we will forget what we really are, as we are replaced by a "common economic management," i.e., a hyperobjective control mechanism. Remember Plato's caution that the greatest danger is our forgetting our true origin—outside the cave.

This Nietzschean vision of a technological nihilism/posthumanism is what Heidegger sees as the first of the primary dangers inherent in the narcissistic and self-defeating humanism expressed by the essence of technology. It is also not difficult to see Nietzsche as prophetic in light of the directions our digital technologies have taken us in the last couple decades. Whether they consciously have Nietzsche in mind, it seems our elites have taken us far in the direction of being dominated by a digital super-man, an alien power. Humanity might give up and accept replacement, leaving our world to be dominated by a mechanical super-humanity that we have set loose. If Anders is correct, Nietzsche's prophecy may have been fulfilled already in 1945.

Heidegger is no humanist, so even human overcoming is not The Danger for him (though we might wonder whether the rest of the world deserves being left to deal with the behemoth we have unwittingly created). This brings us to the second, and primary, danger Heidegger worries that the essence of technology poses:

> The threat to man does not come in the first instance from the potentially lethal machines and apparatus of technology. The actual threat has already affected man in his essence. The rule of Enframing threatens man with the possibility that it could be denied him to enter into a more original revealing and hence to experience the call of a more primal truth. (QT, p. 28)

The Danger, for Heidegger, is that the essence of technology leaves us oblivious to other ways Being might be revealed. Our technological interpretation of being is self-serving; it reveals beings in terms of how they are *accessible to us*. We select out of the indefinite complexity based on which beings are such that we can deal with them. Thus, when we look at the world, as long as we look through a technological lens, we are always partly seeing ourselves reflected back.

That technological lens is increasingly, if not now utterly, the only window we have on the world. We force the world to play by our rules, if we are going to encounter it at all. That is, in some sense, inevitable, i.e., we can only experience what *we* can experience. Nevertheless, the temptation of the essence of technology is to believe that ours is the only way to frame things. The technological interpretation of being does reveal things, and it is highly effective by its standards. These virtues make it difficult, if not impossible, for those of us whose minds have been formed in such terms even to entertain that there might be another way in which a world could come into the light.

Surely, as we have discussed, there are other framings of things, other possibilities for caves or relevance and meaning. But the illusion of the completeness of the technological vision closes us off to anything new, or even primordially old, that might fall outside our technological purview. Maybe there is more that can be in our *Umwelt* than what can be manipulated and controlled (or understood in terms amenable in those ways), but we have closed ourselves off to it by our recent technological obsessions. Maybe there are things from outside our cave that are subtly trying to awaken us to their ambiguous presence. If something wanted to reach out to us (from beyond our cave as it is currently constituted), we simply would not be able to take the call. We are only concerned with what we can manipulate or control, which in principle entails that we are not open to communication from anything higher. Thus, because we are oblivious to any other interpretation of Being, we are trapped in the essence of technology, but as we have seen Heidegger argue at length, that is ultimately a self-undermining piece of narcissism.

Heidegger is not a luddite; he is not looking to turn back the clock to the good old days of wooden bridges and simple windmills. He realizes that the essence of technology has revealed much to us that is of great value, and in any event there is no getting the genie back in the bottle: "It would be foolish to attack technology blindly. It would be shortsighted to condemn it as the work of the devil. We depend on technical devices; they even challenge us to ever greater advances."[181]

Heidegger also thinks it is foolish to believe that *we* are going to find a solution to this problem, The Problem: "Human activity can never directly counter this danger. Human achievement alone can never banish it. But human reflection can ponder the fact that all saving power must be of a higher essence than what is endangered though at the same time kindred to it" (QT, p. 33-34). That is, since the key source of our entrapment by technology is our delusion that we are running things, the idea that we can save ourselves by some even greater technological innovation or revolution in culture or politics is to go all the deeper into the humanistic hubris that is ironically binding us to the Promethean rock![182]

Furthermore, we did not consciously think our way into the predicament. There was no mass committee meeting in the sixteenth century at which humanity collectively decided that we would frame the world in terms of accessibility to our calculative thought processes. History is our doing, but it is equally something that happens to us. We have come to look at

---

[181] Heidegger, "Memorial Address," p. 53.

[182] Certainly, Heidegger's own odious political foibles do much to make this point in the concrete.

Being in a technological way partly because Being has shown itself in a technological way. Taking full responsibility for the situation is, for Heidegger, just one more humanist fantasy. We didn't find our way into this mess, and we are not going to find our way out either. Any saving power must be "kindred to us," but it must be "a higher essence," something beyond us. We cannot save ourselves, and this is what Heidegger means when he says "Only a god can save us." Our attempts to fix our situation are just further expressions of our idolatrous self-worship.

Yet, in this great danger, Heidegger does believe there is hope, a saving power. In fact, he thinks that saving power is only a possibility from within the danger. Even more than usual, Heidegger is cryptic on this point:

> *Only what is granted endures. That which endures primarily out of the earliest beginning is what grants.* (QT, p. 31)

> As destining, the coming to presence of technology gives man entry into That which of himself, he can neither invent nor in any way make. For there is no such thing as a man who, solely of himself, is only man." (QT, p. 31)

> Thus, the coming to presence of technology harbors in itself what we least suspect, the possible arising of the saving power." (QT, p. 32)

Again, that is all less than transparent. On my reading, when Heidegger says that technology is a "destining," he is emphasizing that we are not in full control of whether we see the world in terms of accessibility and exploitation; that is something we "neither invent nor in any way make."

Notice, however, that once we admit that we are destined *by something else* to see the world technologically, we have implicitly renounced the technological stance. We've admitted that, after all, we are not really the ones running things. It is not our doing or choice that has put us in this situation. There is something that does not happen on our own terms, i.e., *that* we insist that the world meet us on our terms is not something that is up to us. The essence of technology happened to us. Paradoxically, to come to realize that we are doomed to believe we control the world is precisely to realize that we are not indeed in control of the world. Destinies and doomings require a power beyond us. Something else is forcing our hands!

We cannot come to this realization without going all the way to the depths of our technological destiny. Only at that low point does it become clear to us that we are in fact suffering through a destiny. But in that dark place we can finally open ourselves to the possibility of something else, because there we must admit it was up to something else that we would end up in such a dire condition. We are thus saved by the openness to contact by that something else, but that can only come once we realize we have been destined to this dangerous situation and remain vigilant in this realization: "Through this we are not yet saved. But we are thereupon summoned to hope in a growing light of the saving power. How can this happen? Here and now in little things, that we may foster the saving power in its increase. This includes holding always before our eyes the extreme danger" (QT, p. 33). The truth will set us free, as it were, because only in that light will we be open to being spoken to by something with a "higher essence." That is to renounce the Promethean bargain without falling into the same trap by the effort.

I realize that our trip through "The Question Concerning Technology" has been a hundred miles of difficult road! Nevertheless, the connections to the UFO phenomenon should be clear. The Heideggerian worry about human overcoming by our own technological obsessions that grow to confront us as a domineering Other resonates with the suggestion I have made in earlier chapters to the effect that The UFO could be a hyperobject that we unwittingly unleashed.

Moreover, that same hyperobjective Other (our Promethean "god") may block us from hearing or seeing other powers that exist on the periphery of our *Umwelt*, i.e., other aspects of Magonia (a broad and ancient hyperobject of which we have been a part for our entire history) are muted by our technological essence. Ufology primarily sees the phenomenon as discrete, nuts-and-bolts pieces of technology, and narrativizes these encounters in an idiom of crash retrievals, reverse engineering, and the possibility of techno-utopia or interplanetary invasion. Those are the kinds of stories that dominate the attention, at the expense of anything else that might be heard from the phenomenon, of those captured by the essence of technology. The very nature of the beings that experiencers encounter are standardly categorized as extraterrestrial, ultraterrestrial, extradimensional or other categories of our techno-science (or pseudoscience) that fit comfortably in the Goldilocks Ontology.

If Strieber is correct, these stories distract us from a "higher essence." Something has indeed been trying to reach us from Magonia, but we don't have eyes to see or ears to hear. As Heidegger predicts, most of us are unwilling to answer Them (to use Strieber's word), because we don't see beyond our framing of things in terms of accessibility to us. We are under the influence of another hyperobject that entraps our attention. The fact that we think of the UFO most naturally in terms of the nuts-and-bolts technology, even as the phenomenon is clearly more uncanny than all that, is symptomatic that our default conditions for thinking (techno-science) are hampering our understanding of the situation.

Nevertheless, those are all points that the previous chapters should have disposed us to see, and I promised an account of the deep connection between Heidegger and Vallée that Pasulka has claimed to be the key to understanding the thought and life of the latter. Consider the following remarks from Vallée's most recent book:

> *What if those UFO devices had been designed so they could not be reverse-engineered by people with our current level of knowledge and social development? What if their target was at a different level? At a symbolic level, about our relationship to life? At a psychic level, about our relationship to the universe? What if they contained an existential warning?*[183]

The Heideggarian stance implied by these questions is clear. Vallée is shifting the *question* of the UFO from the *nuts-and-bolts* to the *existential* level, from the narrow worry about the devices to a more fundamental question of the essence of the UFO. Vallée suggests, albeit obliquely, that there is a message in the phenomenon revealed from our very inability to master it technologically or even understand it in terms of our techno-science, and that message is cautionary ("an existential warning"). Here we have a case of Vallée's concern, *a la* Heidegger, about our narrow techno-scientific stance blinding us from the message we are being sent by something beyond our *Umwelt*, a "god" who might save us from ourselves. Moreover, the existential message of the UFO, for Vallée, is a message about us, our *existence*, much like Heidegger's use of interpretation of the essence of technology as a clue to our being.

These remarks come from *Trinity*, a text in which Vallée recounts in great detail an encounter with a UFO that closely followed (both geographically and temporally) the first explosion of a nuclear device in New Mexico. Indeed, the figures of Oppenheimer and other scientists captured by the Manhattan Project loom throughout the volume. Oppenheimer's quotation "I am the Killer of Worlds" casts its shadow over key moments in *Trinity*: "*Notice the plural? Not just this particular world . . . All the worlds . . .* I feel profound respect for the power of scientific developments, but I dread the possible implications."[184]

Moreover, the true stars of *Trinity* are the two young boys who seem to have witnessed the crash of a craft and the subsequent retrieval of it and its occupants. These boys, who we meet as old men, were part of forgotten communities of people living around the test site that were subjected to the radioactive yield of the bomb. Vallée is keen to observe that the bomb was not so much tested at Trinity as it was deployed on a human population. Great destructive power was put in our hands, and it was callously released on the

---

[183] Jacque F. Vallée and Paola Leopizzi Harris, *Trinity: The Best Kept Secret* (Mansfield, MA: Starworks, 2022), p. 307. The authors' emphasis. Unless otherwise indicated all references are to places in Trinity that are clearly attributed to Vallée.

[184] Harris, *Trinity*, p. 233. Author's emphasis.

very people it was supposedly devised to protect. On top of that subjugation, the boys witness an uncanny event that defies their sense-making abilities, and which haunts ever after their lives. The book, and I believe we can see this motif throughout much of what Vallée writes, is an ironic history of people who have been captured and victimized by a hyperobjective reality that humanity has set in motion.

The test of the bomb was more than the introduction of a terrible weapon into the hands of human beings whose spiritual maturity clearly is not up to the task of managing such power. Rather, the test was the end of a world and a beginning of a new one, "A big transition: The Atomic Age. Everybody takes it for granted now. Ancient history."[185]

There is a worry about our Promethean delusions of omnipotence, and their inevitable backfiring on us, that percolates throughout *Trinity*. In this light, Vallée invites us to see Oppenheimer in a Heideggarian light: an ironic character who opens us up to something speaking beyond our narrow technological obsessions by revealing our grim destiny determined by those very same obsessions as he himself prosecutes their demands. Because Oppenheimer went all the way, he, in his very person, demonstrates to us our greatest danger. We have lost sight of anything else, and in doing so we can see that our delusions of omnipotence are self-refuting. At the same time, Oppenheimer's life hints at a saving power, given his resignation to the inevitability of our nuclear destiny. He reminds us that we are not, after all, really running things in this world, and this ironic anti-humanism opens the way for *something else* to reveal itself.

Vallée is keenly aware of how our now dominant means of sense-making (the essence of technology) occludes as much as it reveals, and he believes that the UFO phenomenon portends something about our coming destiny. We are being spoken to, but Vallée worries that we are unlikely to learn anything from our encounters with the UFO

> as long as our studies, overt or secret, only concern themselves with overt technology on the scene, as staged for our benefit, and framed for our physics . . . . Instead, we believe it is trying to teach us to transcend our own humanity. Or perish in a toxic mental cloud of our own making, when our civilization reaches its point of singularity.[186]

In other words, our technological obsessions with reproduction and control (the essence of technology) limit us to thinking about the phenomenon in the Goldilocks Ontology of our techno-science. Before we can hear what we are being told, we need to leave those limitations of our thought aside (however

---

[185] Vallée, *Trinity*, p. 232.
[186] Vallée, *Trinity*., p. 227.

much they enable us and reveal beings for us), and that is a call to "transcend our humanity"—the nigh impossible task of looking outside the cave. Unless we take up that arduous burden of re-thinking our thinking, we will remain ignorant of a vast world, the *Uber-Umwelt*, that is trying to make itself available to us. Such a cognitive reorientation is our only chance to save ourselves from ourselves. Vallée, along with Heidegger, worries that the essence of technology has made us oblivious to Being, and we need to learn to listen again.

Notice that in the passage I quote directly above, Vallée articulates the danger of our oblivion not as nuclear annihilation (though he's not unconcerned about that!), but "a toxic mental cloud of our making." The danger threatens our *mentality*, our *thinking*. Vallée worries that we are on a road to *perishing* as beings capable of questioning ourselves, and claims that this will come "when our civilization reaches its point of singularity." The danger, for Vallée, is that we will be undermined as distinctively human thinkers (self-conscious and self-critical) by the much-prophesied technological singularity.

Vallée, like Heidegger, anticipates the Nietzschean technological super-man poised to replace us with a mechanical hyperobject disburdened of the irritations of self-consciousness. There are hints in *Trinity* of Anders' post-humans incorporated as parts into a conscienceless and unreflective mechanical hyperobject. Once again in a Heideggarian vein, Vallée seems to take this as the emergent danger that is at least equally as threatening as nuclear annihilation. Either way, humanity is going to be extinct. The incorporation into the Nietzschean machine is so insidious, as it exploits our own technological way of *being-in-the-world* and masks itself in the conditions of our thinking. Prometheus is a cunning deity. Our very sense of human progress is going to euthanize humanity painlessly in a poisonous mental cloud.

Consider how all these themes come together in these remarks from Vallée:

> Everything about the event of the UFO crash at Trinity: its timing, the extraordinary secret surprise it created, the persistent interest of American military Intelligence in its minute details, the long silence of the witnesses, even the specific place where it crashed and the visions it projected, all that has sunk into the unconscious of a human environment obsessed with progress and power—a human environment thoroughly distracted and confused by the new electronic media that have come to define reality— and replace it for our contemporaries.[187]

---

[187] Vallée, *Trinity*, p. 312.

Vallée's suggestion that the "new electronic media' are replacing reality for our contemporaries is telling. *Our world* is increasingly a bath of digitized fantasies we are imposing on ourselves, the pseudo-reality that we put on for our own consumption. Our narcissistic pretensions, with the rise of digital media, have indeed trapped us in a self-imposed simulation, though one that really signifies *nothing*. That is why we can no longer hear what Magonia tells us; we cannot see anything beyond our simulacrum.

Remember, as Pasulka points out in her preface to *American Cosmic*, Vallée is one of the pioneers of the digital age, both as a researcher involved in the early development of the internet and as a venture capitalist funding technology.[188] He, like Oppenheimer, played a role in unleashing a beast that he worries will threaten our demise. There is something analogous to Oppenheimer's "I am become death" in Vallée's ufological writings. Oppenheimer's "destroyer of worlds" is a threat of literal physical destruction, whereas for Vallée the danger is primarily the destruction of the real world as a concern of ours, a final cognitive suicide by a retreat into electronically mediated fantasies (which includes much of ufology). We are sealing ourselves into the cave by blocking the exit digitally, and Pasulka documents the unfolding of that process brilliantly in *American Cosmic*. No doubt, our abdication of the privilege of concern over the real meaning of Being carries with it risks of physical destruction, too, as we are submitting ourselves to control by a mechanical super-man that is beyond concerns or conscience. That is the price of liberation from the anxieties of human existence.

Remember that Heidegger finds the possibility of salvation within the greatest danger. The grave threat is the oblivion that comes along with our capture by the essence of technology. Nevertheless, by conceding that we are subjected to a grim destiny that was not our choosing, we admit that we are not the masters of the universe after all, and that humility is the step toward our being saved by something else that might be speaking to us.

Vallée, as we have discussed earlier, will go no further in his ontology of the UFO than to identify it as a *control mechanism*. He sees in the UFO the message that we are not in complete control of our cognitive lives, and that is the The Message of the UFO. Vallée shares Heidegger's anti-humanism inasmuch as he sees in the UFO a sign that humanity does not have exclusive control over its destiny; our thinking is controlled by some "higher essence." The UFO, which comes to us in our greatest self-imposed danger, can inspire in us the humility to listen again to what Magonia may have to tell us. Thus, Vallée seems to take the UFO as a sign of both our greatest danger and our only hope. The latter, however, can speak to us, only if we learn the hard lessons of humility.

---

[188] Pasulka, *American Cosmic*, p. x.

CONCLUSION

"But 'that world' is well concealed from humans – that dehumanized inhuman world which is a heavenly nothing; and the belly of being does not speak to humans at all, except as a human."

—Friedrich Nietzsche, *Thus Spoke Zarathustra*[189]

"Human motives sharpen all our questions, human satisfactions lurk in all our answers, all our formulas have a human twist . . . Not being reality, but only our belief about reality, it will contain human elements, but these will know the non-human element, in the only sense in which there can be knowledge of anything . . . . Just as impossible may it be to separate the real from the human factors in the growth of our cognitive experience."

William James, *Pragmatism*[190]

So where have we ended up? We began our discussion with Sellars' presentation of the philosophical enterprise as the attempt to create a synoptic vision, a view of the whole that fits all the puzzle pieces together. For Sellars, this knowing our way around the whole in a "reflective way" (a way that actively makes sense of things, as opposed to an encounter with a bunch of

---

[189] Friedrich Nietzsche, *Thus Spoke Zarathustra*, in *The Portable Nietzsche*, trans. and ed. Walter Kaufmann (New York: Penguin, 1954), p. 144.
[190] William James, *Pragmatism*, in *Writings: 1902-1910* (The American Literary Library: New York, 1987), p. 592, 596.

brute facts) is central to what it means to be distinctively human. We don't just get around the world, but we ask why our ways of getting around make sense, not just to ourselves, but to *anyone* else. This is what Socrates means when pointed out to his fellow Athenians that the unexamined life is not worth living.

I fear, however, the UFO is a very stout wrench that has been thrown into these works. At this point, I believe we cannot deny that the UFO, nor the host of other super natural entities that beguiled us, have a place in human experience. Even if one is a UFO anti-realist, then she needs to account for why this particular delusion has become so powerfully captivating to so many human beings across the globe in a relatively short period of time. That we can fall into mass delusion on such a scale is a significant datum for our self-understanding, and that realization should lead us to a certain skepticism toward our own beliefs: What else are we apt to trick ourselves into believing?

Moreover, none of that leaves the question of why we are assailed by the UFO delusion, as opposed to other supposed fantasies, at this point in history, which is itself an important question, the answer to which is far from transparent. In short, even UFO anti-realism leaves us with stark realizations. That being said, I believe UFO anti-realism is no longer sustainable, and the reality of the UFO does not fit comfortably in our overall ontological mosaic, at least not yet, and maybe it never will.

As we have learned along the way, the fact that the UFO doesn't fit into our puzzle has as much to do with our limitations as it does with the recalcitrance of the phenomenon. My way of trying to fit the UFO piece into the picture has been to lower our expectations for completing the puzzle. The problem with the UFO isn't the UFO, but our impatience, anxieties, needs, and pretensions to the will to power, all of which are likely non-negotiable parts of our nature. It is the human condition that blocks the way to understanding the UFO.

Surely, you have noticed that we get in our own way with respect to much more than the UFO. The phenomenon is merely the case we have studied in detail in these pages, but the difficulties we have repeatedly encountered can be generalized. The human condition, our dependence on our cave-dwelling limitations, blocks us from a transparent understanding of the world. However hard we look, our vision is partly distorted by our own reflection. Thus, it is not only the philosophical inquiry into the UFO that is left incomplete, but the philosophical endeavor in general. We should see our frustrations in understanding the UFO as a sign of the human condition. We don't get the synoptic view of the whole, because *our view* is always *our view*.

As we discussed, even the founder of the discipline of philosophy, Plato, does not promise us anything better. He sees the prospect of a completed philosophy as something that comes only with a sort of death, a complete transcendence of the conditions of human living. Until such time, we can only remember, but recollection is not something within our power. The value of our philosophical encounter with the UFO is then the revelation of our own limitations; it shows us that a completed philosophy is an ideal, and not a concrete reality, because there is something lurking just outside our cave that defies our comprehension.

Do we then end on a dire note? I don't have anything to hedge against a certain Sisyphean fate, wherein we are perpetually left to ask questions that forever remain beyond our cognitive paygrade. We don't get a picture of things that is not partially obscured by our own reflection. At least in this life or under our own power, the proverbial "God's eye view" of what is beyond the cave is not our privilege. Even if we share the lot of Sisyphus, that does not mean there is no promise in this self-discovery. Maurice Merleau-Ponty has something like this in mind:

> But what if it were precisely the case that the order of facts invaded the order of values, if it were recognized that dichotomies are tenable only this side of a certain point of misery and danger? Even those among us today who are taking up the word "humanism" again no longer maintain the *shameless humanism* of our elders. What defines our time is perhaps to dissociate humanism from the idea of a humanity fully guaranteed by natural law, and not only to reconcile the consciousness of human values and the consciousness of the infrastructures which keep them in existence, but insist upon their inseparability.[191]

Merleau-Ponty writes those remarks at the end of an account of our cave-dwelling status; "the order of facts invaded the order of values," i.e., circumstances beyond our control frame what we value and what we take as meaningful. He does not, however, see this as an occasion to despair, but as our reaching a sort of spiritual maturity. We are getting over the arrogance of our "shameless humanism," which brings "misery and danger." In other words, even if humility forces us to realize our Sisyphean situation, it finally absolves us of our Faustian bargain with Prometheus.

Our study of the UFO on a philosophical plane is one of the most promising prospects on offer for us to reach this honest assessment of our condition. Maybe the UFO can jog our memory of the world of the dead, now when we need to recollect the most.

---

[191] Maurice Merleau-Ponty, "Man and Adversity," in *The Merleau-Ponty Reader*, trans. and ed. T. Toadvine and L. Lawlor (Evanston, IL: Northwestern University Press, 2007), p. 191. Merleau-Ponty's emphasis.

ACKNOWLEDGEMENTS

I have many people to thank for helping me to bring this project to fruition, though none of its shortcomings are their fault. Were it not for Diana Pasulka's example and direct encouragement, I would never have entered into serious study of the UFO phenomenon. I have learned much from her both about this field of study and academic life in general. Kelly Chase has been generous to me by allowing me to develop a lot of these ideas on her superb podcast, *The UFO Rabbit Hole*, and her own deep thinking and scholarship have taught me a great deal. I am also grateful for her editorial assistance and encouragement to throw my hat into ufology. I have been blessed to gain these two outstanding women as friends through this process. Speaking of outstanding women, thanks are due to my wife, Jennifer, for tolerating my new obsession with the UFO. My children have also spent dozens of hours listening to UFO podcasts with me. There are far worse mid-life crises to suffer through with your husband and father, but this one, I am sure, has its special burdens. I also appreciate the openness my students showed to these ideas, including some truly discomforting implications. Their willingness both to let me think aloud and to challenge me in the classroom helped hone my thinking. and in particular I am thankful for conversations with Rose Johnson (possibly "the brightest witch of her age") and Adam Wilbur. Finally, I am grateful to you, the reader of this book, for giving me an opportunity to share my ideas with a wider audience.

BIBLIOGRAPHY

Aeschylus. *Prometheus Bound*, translated by Deborah Roberts. Indianapolis, IN: Hackett, 2012.

Anders, Gunther. "Reflections on the H-Bomb." *Dissent*. Spring 1956.

---------- "Promethean Shame." In *Promethean Shame: Technology, Digital Culture, and Human Obsolescence*, translated by Christopher John Miller. New York: Rowan & Littlefield 2016.

Arendt, Hannah. *Eichmann in Jerusalem: A Report on the Banality of Evil*. New York: Penguin, 2007.

Aristotle, *Categories*. In *The Complete Works of Aristotle* Vol. 1. Princeton, NJ: Princeton University Press, 1984.

---------- *Physics*, in *The Complete Works of Aristotle*, Vol. 1 Princeton, NJ: Princeton University Press, 1984.

----------- *Metaphysics*, translated by W.D. Ross. In *The Complete Works of Aristotle* Vol. 2. Princeton, NJ: Princeton University Press, 1984.

----------- *Metaphysics*. Translated by C.D.C. Reeve. Indianapolis, Indiana: Hackett Publishing Company, 2016.

---------- *Politics*, translated by . C.D.C. Reeve. Indianapolis, Indiana: Hackett Publishing, 2017.

---------- *Aristotle's Theology: The Primary Texts*. Edited and Translated by C.D.C. Reave. Indianapolis, IN: Hackett Publishing) 2023.

Austin, J.L. *Sense and Sensibilia*. New York: Oxford University Press, 1962.

Browning, Christopher. *Ordinary Men: Reserve Police Battalion 101 and the Final Solution in Poland*. New York: Harper, 2017.

Clark, Andy. *Being There: Putting Brain, Body, and World Together*.Cambridge, MA: Bradford Books, 1997.

Clark, Andy and Chalmers, David. "The Extended Mind." *Analysis* 58.1 (1998), 7–19.

Coulthart, Ross. *In Plain Sight: An Investigation into UFOs and Impossible Science*. New York: Harper, 2012.

Crawford, Matthew. *The World Beyond Your Head: On Becoming an Individual in an Age of Distraction*. New York: Farrar, Strauss, and Giroux, 2016.

Dennett, Daniel. *Darwin's Dangerous Idea*. New York: Simon and Schuster, 1996.

Desmett, Mattias. *The Psychology of Totalitarianism*. White River Junction, VT: Chelsea Green Publishing, 2022.

Dostoevsky, Fyodor. *The Grand Inquisitor with Related Chapters from The Brothers Karamazov*, translated by Constance Garnett. Indianapolis, IN: Hackett Publishing, 1993.

Dreyfus, Hubert, and Taylor, Charles. *Retrieving Realism*. Cambridge, MA: Harvard University Press, 2015.

Dreyfus, Hubert. *What Computers Still Can't Do: A Critique of Artificial Reason*. Cambridge, MA: MIT Press, 1982.

Ellul, Jacques. *The Technological Society*, translated by John Wilkinson. New York: Vintage, 1964.

Latour, Bruno. *We Have Never Been Modern*, translated by Catherine Porter. Cambridge, MA: 1993.

Goff, Phillip. *Galileo's Error: Foundations for a New Science of* Consciousness. New York: Vintage, 2009.

Harman, Graham. *Tool Being: Heidegger and the Metaphysics of Objects*.Chicago: Open Court, 2002.

---------- *The Quadruple Object*. New York: Zero Books, 2011.

---------- "Aristotle with a Twist." *Speculative Medievalisms: Discography*, 2013: 227-254.

---------- *Immaterialism: Objects and Social Theory*. New York: Polity, 2016.

---------- *Object Oriented Ontology: A New Theory of Everything*.New York: Pelican, 2018).

Haugland, John. *Dasein Disclosed: John Haugeland's Heidegger*, edited by Joseph Rouse. Cambridge, MA: Harvard University Press, 2013.

Heidegger, Martin. *Being and Time*. Translated by John Macquarrie and Edward Robinson. New York: Harper Collins, 1962.

----------"The Memorial Address." In *Discourse on Thinking*, 43–57. Translated by J. Anderson and E. Freund. New York: Harper, 1966.

----------"The Question Concerning Technology." In *The Question Concerning Technology and Other Essays*, 3-35. Translated by William Levitt. New York: Harper, 1977.

----------"The Word of Nietzsche 'God is Dead'." In *The Question Concerning Technology and Other Essays*, 53–114. Translated by William Levitt. New York: Harper 1977.

---------- *What is Called Thinking?* Translated by Glenn Gray. New York: Harper, 1976.

Husserl, Edmund. *The Crisis of European Sciences*, translated by David Carr. Evanston Illinois: Northwestern University Press, 1970.

James, William. *The Will to Believe and Other Popular Essays*, in *Writings: 1878-1899, 445-704*. New York: Literary Classics of the United States, 1992.

---------- *A Pluralistic Universe*. In *Writings: 1902-1910, 625-820*. New York: Literary Classics of the United States, 1987

John Keel, *Operation Trojan Horse: The Classic Breakthrough Study of UFOs*. San Antonio, TX: Anomalist Press, 1970/2013.

Jung, C.J. *On the Nature of Psyche*, translated by R.F.C. Hull. Princeton, NJ: Princeton University Press, 1960.

--------- *Flying Saucers: A Modern Myth of Things Seen in the Skies*, translated by R.F.C. Hull. Princeton, N.J.: Princeton University Press, 1978.

Kastrup, Bernardo. *More Than Allegory: On Religious Myth, Truth, and Belief.* New York: IFF Books, 2016.

---------- *The Idea of the Word: A Multi-Disciplinary Argument for the Mental Nature of Reality.* New York: IFF Books, 2019.

Kripal, Jeffrey. *Superhumanities: Historical Precedents, Moral Objections, and New Realities.* Chicago: University of Chicago Press, 2022.

Lear, Jonathan. *Aristotle: The Desire to Understand.* New York: Cambridge, 1988.

Loeb, Paul S. *The Death of Nietzsche's Zarathustra.* New York: Cambridge University Press, 2012.

Madden, James D. *Thinking About Thinking: Mind and Meaning in the Age of Technological Nihilism* (Eugen, Oregon: Cascade, 2023).

Merleau-Ponty, Maurice. "Man and Adversity." In *The Merleau-Ponty Reader,* edited and translated by Toadvine and L. Lawlor, 189-240. Evanston, IL: Northwestern University Press, 2009.

---------- *The Phenomenology of Perception.* Translated by Donald A. Landes. New York, Routledge, 2012.

Milgram, Stanley. *Obedience to Authority: An Experimental View.* New York: Harper, 2009.

Morton, Timothy. *Hyperobjects: Philosophy and Ecology at the End of the World.* Minneapolis, MN: University of Minnesota Press, 2013.

Nietzsche, Friedrich. *Thus Spoke Zarathustra.* In *The Portable Nietzsche,* transalted and edited by Walter Kaufmann. New York: Penguin, 1954.

---------- *The Birth of Tragedy,* translated by Francis Goffling. New York: Anchor Books, 1956.

---------- *The Genealogy of Morals,* translated by Francis Golffling. New York: Anchor Books, 1956.

---------- *Will to Power,* translated by W. Kaufmann and R. Hollingdale. New York: Vintage, 1967.

Nussbaum, *The Fragility of Goodness: Luck and Ethics in Greek Tragedy and Ethics.* Cambridge: Cambridge University Press, 2001.

Pasulka, Diana. *American Cosmic: UFOs, Technology, Religion.* New York, Oxford University Press, 2019.

--------- *Encounters: Experiences with Nonhuman Intelligences.* St. Martin's: New York, 2023.

--------- "A Tour of Silicon Valley with Jacques Vallée," Draft: https://www.academia.edu/34657465/A_Tour_of_Silicon_Valley_with_Jacques_Vallée (accessed 5/15/23).

Putoff, H.E. "Ultraterrestrial Models." *The Journal of Cosmology* Vol. 29, No. 1: https://thejournalofcosmology.com/Puthoff.pdf (accessed, May 21, 2023).

Plato, *Phaedo.* Translated by G.M.A. Grube. In *Plato: Complete Works,* 49-100. Edited by John Cooper. Indianapolis, IN: Hackett Publishing, 1987.

--------- *Republic.* Translated by C.D.C. Reeve. Indianapolis, IN: Hackett, 2004.

\-\-\-\-\-\-\-\-\- *Timaeus* in *Timaeus and Critias*, translated by T.K. Johansen. New York: Penguin, 1965.

Quine, W.V.O. "Two Dogmas of Empiricism." In *From Logical Point of View*. Cambridge, MA: Harvard University Press, 1980.

Ratzinger, Joseph. *Introduction to Christianity*. San Francisco, CA: Ignatius Press, 2003.

Reeve, C.D.C. *Aristotle: A Quick Emersion*. New York: Tibidabo Publishing, 2019.

Rojcewicz, Richard. *Heidegger, Plato, Philosophy, Death: An Atmosphere of Mortality*. New York: Rowan and Littlefield, 2021.

Sheldrake, Rupert. "Is the Sun Conscious?" *The Journal of Consciousness Studies* 20, No. 2-4, 2020: 8-28

Sellars, Wilfrid. "Philosophy and the Scientific Image of Man." In *Science, Perception, and Reality*, 1-35. Atascadero, CA: Ridgeview Publishing, 1991.

Strieber, Whitely, and Kripal, Jeffrey. *The Super Natural: Why the Unexplained is Real*. New York: Tarcher Perigee, 2016.

Streiber, Whitely. *Them*. San Antonio, TX: Walker and Collier, 2023.

Sullivan, Thomas and Menssen, Sandra. *The Agnostic Inquirer: Revelation from a Philosophical Standpoint*. Grand Rapids, MI: Eerdmans, 2007.

Taylor, Charles. *A Secular Age*. Cambridge, MA: Belknap Press, 2008.

Taylor, Kathleen *Brainwashing: The Science of Thought Control*. New York: Oxford University Press, 2017.

Thompson, Evan. "Life and Mind: From Autopoesis to Neurophenomenology." *Phenomenology and Cognitive Science*, 2 (2004): 381-398.

\-\-\-\-\-\-\-\-\-\-\- *Mind in Life: Biology, Phenomenology, and the Sciences of Mind*. Cambridge, MA: Harvard University Press, 2007.

Tomasello, Michael. *A Natural History of Human Thinking*. Cambridge, MA: Harvard, 2014.

Vallée, Jacques, and Harris, Paola. *Trinity: The Best Kept Secret* (Mansfield, MA: Starworks Publishing, 2022

Vallée, Jacques. *The Invisible College: What a Group of Scientists Has Discovered About UFO Influence on the Human Race*. San Antonio, TX: Anomalist Books, 1975.

\-\-\-\-\-\-\-\-\- *Messengers of Deception: UFO Contacts and Cults*. Brisbane, Australia: Daily Grail Publishing, 2008

\-\-\-\-\-\-\-\-\- *Revelations: Alien Contact and Human Deception*. San Antonio: Anomalist Books, 2015.

von Hippel, William. *The Social Leap: The New Evolutionary Science of Who We Are, Where We Come From, and What Makes us Happy*. New York: Harper Wave, 2018.

Wittgenstein, Ludwig. *Tratatus Logicus-Philosophicus*, translated by C.K. Ogden. In *Major Works: Selected Philosophical Writings*. New York: Harper, 2009.

----------- *Philosophical Investigations*, translated by G.E.M. Anscombe, P.M.S. Hacker, and J. Schulte. Oxford: Blackwell, 2009.

Yong, Ed. *An Immense World*. New York: Random House, 2022.

INDEX

ABOUT THE AUTHOR

James D. Madden is a professor of philosophy at Benedictine College. He is the author of *Unidentified Flying Hyperobject: UFOs, Philosophy, and the End of the World* (Ontocalypse 2023), *Thinking About Thinking: Mind and Meaning in the Era of Techno-Nihilism* (Cascade, 2023), and *Mind, Matter, and Nature* (CUA, 2013), along with scholarly articles on the philosophy of mind and the philosophy of religion. You can find out more about his work at jdmadden.com.

Made in United States
Troutdale, OR
12/15/2023

15936049R00086